FAIRFIELD FOLK

A History of the British Fairground and its People

FRANCES BROWN

HALSGROVE

Dedicated to the memory of my parents
Harry & Louie Stroud

and to my late husband
Henry Anthony Brown

First published in Great Britain in 2012

Copyright © 2012 Frances Brown

British Library Cataloguing-in-Publication Data
A CIP record for this title is available from the British Library

ISBN 978 0 85704 156 2

HALSGROVE
Halsgrove House,
Ryelands Business Park,
Bagley Road, Wellington, Somerset TA21 9PZ
Tel: 01823 653777   Fax: 01823 216796
email: sales@halsgrove.com

Part of the Halsgrove group of companies
Information on all Halsgrove titles is available at: www.halsgrove.com

Printed in China by Everbest Printing Co Ltd

CONTENTS

RELATIONSHIP OF MAIN CHARACTERS

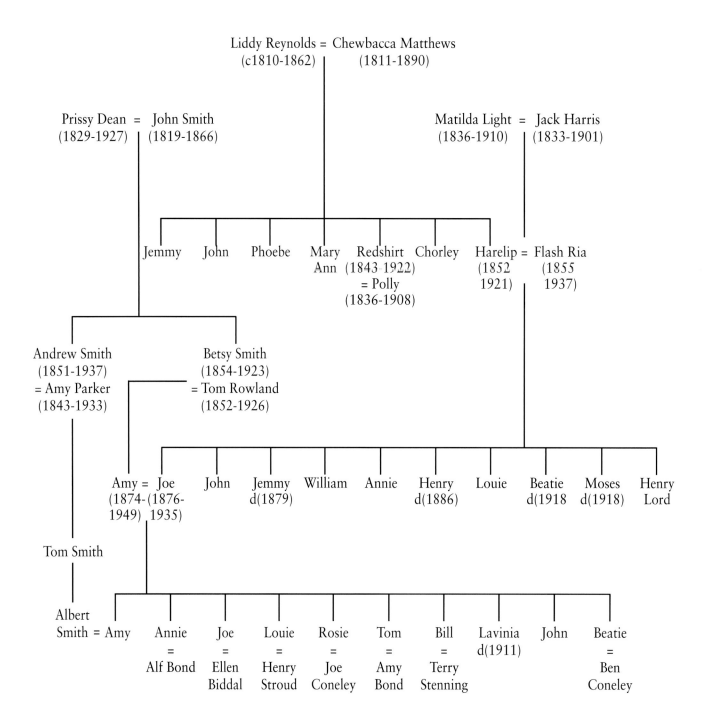

Liddy Reynolds = Chewbacca Matthews
(c1810-1862)   (1811-1890)

Prissy Dean = John Smith
(1829-1927) (1819-1866)

Matilda Light = Jack Harris
(1836-1910)   (1833-1901)

Jemmy   John   Phoebe   Mary   Redshirt   Chorley   Harelip = Flash Ria
                            Ann   (1843-1922)   (1852   (1855
                                   = Polly   1921)   1937)
                                   (1836-1908)

Andrew Smith   Betsy Smith
(1851-1937)   (1854-1923)
= Amy Parker   = Tom Rowland
(1843-1933)   (1852-1926)

Amy = Joe   John   Jemmy   William   Annie   Henry   Louie   Beatie   Moses   Henry
(1874-(1876-   d(1879)   d(1886)   d(1918   d(1918   Lord
1949) 1935)

Tom Smith

Albert
Smith = Amy   Annie   Joe   Louie   Rosie   Tom   Bill   Lavinia   John   Beatie
               =   =   =   =   =   =   d(1911)   =
               Alf Bond Ellen Henry   Joe   Amy   Terry   Ben
                        Biddal Stroud   Coneley Bond   Stenning   Coneley

INTRODUCTION

On summer Sundays during my childhood we sometimes visited Granny – if, that is, we knew where to find her. Was she still at Newhaven near the jetty, or in the Dripping Pan at Lewes? Or had she moved on already to Lindfield Common? Occasionally we arrived to find a meadow with only yellowing patches and circles to betray that here recently had stood wheel-'em-ins, hooplas, rides and sideshows. Surveying battered grass and tyre ruts by the gate, we knew we had just missed her.

When the calendar showed the date of some traditional fair we set off with no misgivings. On arrival we would see her 'stuff' all built up, still and silent under laced-up tilts; empty packing trucks, lorries and living-wagons pulled round the periphery as if anticipating attack from Red Indians. In pride of place a cream-coloured wagon with diamond-paned windows, and leaning over the lower half of its double door, Granny.

My parents were travellers who had settled down just before I was born. As time passed, and especially after my grandmother's death, our links with the fairground fraternity wore thin.

The first years of my married life were spent in London and, when we eventually moved to the country, we chose Haywards Heath simply for its fast commuter line. As newcomers to the area, we had no special interest in the row that blew up over the council's proposal to annex a strip of the cemetery for its road-widening scheme. Many local people, however, were outraged when they heard that several graves were about to be disturbed.

'Can't say I feel much sympathy for them,' I remarked to my husband. 'After all, if the families concerned have neglected the graves for so long, they shouldn't complain now if the council wants to move them.'

'Still,' he objected, 'it is consecrated ground.'

One day my son ran eagerly home from school with news. 'Mum, Mum, the fair's come. It's in the park. Can we go?' Of course, there was no resisting. Daniel drove his sister wildly around in the dodgems. Then both children grew impatient as I chatted at length to the man in the Darts' stall, but cheered up over lemonade and cake in their great-uncle's wagon.

'Did you know,' Uncle Tom asked, 'your great-great-grandparents are buried in the churchyard over the road? I'm talking about your great-granny's mother and father. Oh yes! Some of the old-timers could still tell the tale of Jack Harris and his wife; big showmen they were in this part of the world. I'm going back a good few years, mind. Old Jack, he was one of the first to travel a set of steam gallopers in the south country. And his daughter, Ria – Flash Ria they used to call her – well, it was her as married your great-grandfather, Harelip Matthews.'

Flash Ria and Harelip? I had never heard of them. Their names, if nothing more, intrigued me. But there was something more ...

A picture came into my mind. Three dark-clothed matriarchs smiled into my eyes as they sat on the edge of a dodgem track. A tiny girl, my eldest sister, stood between my mother and grandmother. On the other side of grandmother sat a tall, well-built old lady wearing a bright blouse, silk scarf and ample pinafore. She had just laid aside her black bonnet but clasped her walking-stick ready to bustle off as soon as the shutter clicked.

I had the photograph at home in an old tin box. After tucking the children into bed that night, I rummaged for it.

Ria Matthews in her eighties, eyes sparkling with mischief. 'Flash Ria' – how had she come by that name? She must have been born in the middle of the last century, and her father, like her husband, was a travelling showman ... but what about his father, and his father's father? Were they all showmen? How far could the tradition be traced back? What connection, if any, did they have with other travelling folk, the gypsies, didikais, hawkers, and tinkers? What had made them take to the road in the first place?

There was no immediate way of answering my questions. A visit to the churchyard was disappointing. I searched in vain for headstones bearing the names of Jack Harris and his wife. The reason became clear when I spoke to the vicar. Together we looked through parish registers for the turn of the century. Yes. John Harris, buried in

February 1901; his wife, Matilda Mary, laid in the same grave, November 1910. But ... their bodies had recently been disinterred and placed under a communal cross.

'You probably remember,' explained the vicar. 'It happened when the council was widening the road.'

Mea culpa! I was one of the neglectful descendants. So soon had ancestors faded into oblivion. Determined to salvage what I could of their story, I visited travellers of the older generation and questioned them about the family. They loved talking about the past; I loved listening to them. Although some of their tales strained credulity, subsequent research in county archives, libraries and newspaper offices confirmed and expanded the truth of what I heard. Only the timescale had become warped. Many incidents 'remembered' and recounted as if they happened the day before yesterday had in fact taken place well over a hundred years ago.

Four generations: Flash Ria, Amy, Louie and Barbara Louisa.

Chapter One

A FIGHTING MUSH

So great a depth of snow had fallen as completely to bury his tent, and he could not perceive the slightest vestige of it, while the face of the country had undergone such a change, that he was unable to find even the spot where his wife and children were literally immured alive.

(*Sussex Advertiser*, 20 February 1837)

Two days before Christmas, 1836, and the weather bitterly cold. Chewbacca Matthews, pedlar, arrived in Ditchling, Sussex, with his family and looked around for the most sheltered spot for their tent. The obvious place was the chalk-pit at the foot of the Bosthill, a steep path winding up over the South Downs.

He set to work quickly, unpacked his ridge pole and slotted flexible withies into the holes down its length to form the tent skeleton. He threw over the top a dingy canvas. Soon the chavvies were able to duck down into the darkness, hugging themselves together for warmth. Liddy, Chewbacca's wife, had already got a fire going. The family would eat well before turning in for the night.

Snow started to fall in the early hours, slow at first, but insistent. It did not deter Chewbacca from setting out alone to trek twenty miles on foot from Ditchling to Horsham. What mission took him away is not known. Maybe there was a challenge fight arranged or some member of his family lay desperately ill. Nothing less would have made him leave Liddy and the chavvies on Christmas Eve.

Her man gone, Liddy, with the baby strapped tightly to her body in a shawl, tramped a mile to the village with a basket full of ribbons and trinkets to sell. Christmas Eve was a good time for bickin; she could count on festive cheer brimming over into generosity, especially towards a poor travelling woman with a babe in arms. Liddy, herself, also had purchases to make. She had to buy more food before the shops closed for the holiday, and she would take money from the 'deep pocket' under her skirt to buy playthings for the chavvies. 'Poor travelling folk' they might be in the eyes of gorgies, but there was no need for her sons to go without on Christmas morning.

The snow was still falling. She must buy something to occupy the chavvies if, perish the thought, the weather was too bad on the morrow for them to spend much time out of the tent.

Meanwhile, in the chalk-pit six-year old Jemmy and his younger brother, under instruction to bring in wood for the fire, romped about in the snow with their dog. So absorbed, they scarcely noticed that the Bosthill had disappeared from view, the track becoming indistinguishable from surrounding hills and fields. Then the dog rushed off a few paces, barking furiously, and there was a man on a horse struggling across the field, shouting and waving at them. Jemmy waded through the whiteness to see what the stranger wanted, quickly thinking was there anything he must be careful to hide.

There was no need for the child to adopt his habitual guise of innocence. The man was simply the local butcher who, having been out with his last Christmas deliveries and accepting a little something at each place of call 'just to keep out the cold', now had lost his way. Jemmy led him to the nearly invisible track and pointed the route towards Ditchling. Before he reached the village the butcher passed Liddy on her way back to the camp. The woman and babe looked half-frozen as they were driven along by the bitter north-east wind beginning to sweep up the snow into ominous drifts.

Christmas morning, 1836; a Sunday. As bells from parish churches peeled out, in Sussex their sound carried with unusual clarity and to distances not normally reached. When the bells ceased, the world returned to unearthly silence, everything in the landscape muffled and shrouded in white.

Chewbacca did not start back from Horsham until first light on the day after Christmas. He was twenty-five years old and had the sort of toughness tempered by battling round after round in bare knuckle fights. He was well used to walking in all weathers. The conditions that morning, though, would have daunted the sternest soul. Roads throughout the southern counties were blocked by banks of solid snow. Unwary travellers risked stumbling into drifts up to twenty feet deep. It was reported later that, when one of the coastguards could not extricate himself from a snowdrift near Bexhill, he drew attention to his plight by letting off the blue flares he happened to be carrying. He was rescued, but there were others less fortunate.

Hurrying along as fast as he could manage, Chewbacca ignored the nagging, inner whisper. "You're mad, dinilow, to do this journey today. Best to have bided till the weather calmed down." The snow had stopped, but all the while the wind, that cutting nor-nor-easterly was raging, and he had to push on into its teeth for much of the way.

Other men had the sense to stay within doors that day. During the whole of the fraught journey he saw scarcely the track of another human being, and as for carts or carriages, it was as though the wheel had not yet been invented. The usual welcoming landmarks had been erased or distorted beyond recognition. If it hadn't been for the church spires, he doubted whether he would have found his way at all, since roads and wastes and fields had merged into dazzling white anonymity. And so he thanked the Lord for each identifiable church tower or spire as it came into view.

Gradually, as he trudged on and on through the hours of the morning, the deadly wind abated. Still silence hung, like a pall, over all the land.

Chewbacca urged himself on relentlessly, a small dark figure against the whiteness, until he came within sight of Ditchling church. He passed through the village and summoned up all his fading strength to manage the last leg of the walk that would bring him to his wife and children in their tent at the foot of the Bosthill.

But - where was the Bosthill?

He looked up at the looming heights of the Downs above him. Their contours had changed. He turned round and looked back along the way he had just come. His tracks led into no-where. He couldn't even see the village from here. Could he have taken the wrong direction? No, he knew this spot so well he couldn't have mistaken the way.

He paced up and down over the crisp surface of snow, looking about him but failing to perceive any vestige of his tent. For a man who had just walked twenty miles in onerous conditions it was almost too much to bear.

"Liddy, Liddy, and my biddi chavvies, for Duveleste, where've you taken yourselves to?"

Then the thought struck him: once Liddy realised how heavy the snow was falling, she would have left the tent and taken the chavvies to shelter in a barn nearby. Of course.

Weary and dispirited, Chewbacca turned back on his tracks, and took a few paces before he remembered the dog. He had left the dog with them. Even if the family was deaf to his shouts, the jukel might hear and respond, so he raised his voice to its utmost and hollered the animal's name. The sound echoed through the muffled stillness. He called again ... and again. Then he heard it, the sound of the dog barking from some deep recess hidden beneath the surface of the snow.

Chewbacca rushed to the spot shouting frantically for Liddy. He could hear her faint voice and also the boys calling, but try as he might he could not penetrate the solid barrier to reach them. Forgetting former exhaustion, he started running, running back to the village to fetch help.

When he returned, it was with several sturdy labourers armed with spades who together dug through the snow until they could free the stricken family.

The *Sussex Advertiser*, 20 February 1837, continues the story:

Not content with having leant their aid to release them apparently from a bed of death, the countrymen conducted (the family) to the village, where they obtained a charitable supply of that warmth and sustenance of which the shivering and starving beings stood in so much need.

One of their most liberal benefactors was the grateful butcher whom Jemmy had conducted into the road after the snow had first begun to fall.

This drama involving a 'gypsy' family took up very

The Snowdrop Inn, Lewes, marks the site of the avalanche.

little space in newspaper columns given over to the nation-wide havoc wreaked by the disastrous winter storm. Less than ten miles down the road from Ditchling in Lewes, the county town, an avalanche of snow crushed and swept away seven houses with the loss of nine lives. As in the fable of the mighty oak and the slender willow, solid houses crumbled while a fragile tent endured. Liddy and her children were spared.

Oral tradition in the Matthews family declares that Liddy, or Lydia Reynolds, also known as Gowan, was not born into the travelling fraternity. Her father was said to be a preacher at Ewell in Surrey and her upbringing one that endowed her with a degree of booklearning as well as practical lacemaking skills. How this young woman met and married a travelling prize-fighter is described in a 'say' still recited:

't were back-end of the year, yer see, and this great sheep fair at Ewell. Wal, thousens 'pon thousens of sheep were brought into it, and there were this pleasure fair held there, too. Jem Mathis was but a young 'un then, mind, an' he comes there special ter challenge the local bully. Thet's how it was then, yer see, Jem Mathis, or Chewbacca as we call 'un, was a prize-fighter. None of the glove fightin', mind, not in them days – fought bare ter 'is waist and wiv knuckles.

And someone would c'leck money for 'em. Yer know, they'd go all round wiv a purse and arsk: Money for the Champ. An' then the local bully, he'd try ter claim that money – but, no – he couldn't have it – not less fust he defeat the champion – an' that were Chewbacca.

Wal, it was Ewell Fair and there's Chewbacca punishin' this local feller when Liddy sets eyes on 'im and knowed straightaway – that's the one she'd marry – an, yer know, no matter her father bein' a preacher an' that an' her bein' a fine Lattin scholar an' all – she'd have her way.

And, do yer know, she made this kushti lace – on a pillar – an' used ter show it orf on the stalls at fairs. And the book-larnin', that was kushti too, an' she taught one of her chavvies ter read from the Bible at her knee. Taught her Chorley ter read 'n write good nor any gorgie, she did.

An' that were Liddy.

At the time when Chewbacca and Liddy met, Ewell boasted two annual fairs, one on 12 May for the sale of cattle, and the other, more important event, on 29 October. The latter was a combined sheep and pleasure fair. About 40,000 sheep were penned each autumn in Ewell. By dawn on fair day, roads leading to the meadow at the corner of Reigate Road were thronged with animals, most of which would change hands before sunset.

Along Main Street and in Green Man Yard stood a long avenue of shows, booths and stalls which sprang into life at noon when the showmen unfurled their pictures, bands began to play, and clowns, dancers, acrobats and jugglers appeared on the platforms. From all the countryside around pleasure-seekers flocked in to enjoy the sights. When darkness fell, lamps flared and candles flickered on the fronts of shows, smaller lights glimmered along the toy and gingerbread stalls, and booths were illuminated with thousands of tiny lamps, sapphire and amber, emerald and ruby, arranged in the form of crowns, stars and feathers.

The merry-making rarely broke up without a fight and Chewbacca Matthews had a reputation for never refusing a challenge. The family 'say' continues:

Ol' Chewbacca was a fighting mush, and no mistake. Champs used ter foller 'im abart from place ter place biden they's chance.

Wal, once he were follered up an' down the country by this mush, name of Light, an' he caught up wiv Chewbacca at Warm'ster. An' when theys two met, Light, he throws 'is 'at on the ground and they begins ter fight. And Light, he'd got this corleyfler ear an' a mooey all ugly wiv' the weltin's he's taken, but, dordy, he's good.

He could fight hard, that mush, an' reerly punish a feller. An' Chewbacca, comes the time he thinks to hissel', "Now I see as I've met me match. This mush has beat me. One last punch is all I've got and then gi's in, stripe me if I don't."

So Chewbacca, he'm thrown that last punch and, do yer know, he'm knocks Light clean out wiv it. Wal, arterwards, they'm two mushes is c'lapsed in chairs in the Pub, so wored out as they carn't even fetch 'emsels drink. But the Landlord, he's 'appy wiv 'em an' waits on 'em like they was lords an' they drinks tergevver nightlong, best 'o pals.

New rules of pugilism were formulated in 1838. Fighters did not yet wear gloves but the size of the ring was standardised at twenty-four feet square contained by eight stakes and two ropes, the higher one four feet from the ground. Such regulations were academic as far as Chewbacca was concerned. He was used to the sort of unruly contest that took place between Jimmy Lee and Tommy Rossiter at Molesey in the late 1830s. Both fighters were travellers nurturing grudges from earlier fairs that season. No stakes were hammered into the ground. Their brethren simply stood, armed with snuffbox sticks and the throwing sticks known as livetts, and held the ring whilst inside the two fighters dashed at each other with bare fists, jabbing, clinching, breaking

Brushes, baskets, and chairs being sold at the fair.

away, grimly persisting round after round until one man no longer had strength to stand.[1]

It was a great day for his family when Chewbacca won a heavy purse, but the children grew up mindful of Liddy's grumbles as she laboured to remove the bloodstains from his smock. Fortunately they were not dependent on pugilism's uncertain rewards for their livelihood.

Chewbacca had been born a 'traveller'. Nothing made him angrier than to be called 'gypsy' – a label mistakenly applied to almost any person travelling the roads in the nineteenth century. As a traveller Chewbacca could turn to any number of rural crafts and fairground activities to make money. He was not afraid of hard work. He mended chairs, made and sold baskets, brushes, pegs, walking-sticks, and toys. He was a horse-dealer, pedlar, hawker and travelling showman. In the 'Hungry Forties' when times were lean for so many in the countryside, he turned to anything on hand to make a living and feed his growing family – always with the exception, of course, of taking a job. Chewbacca Matthews was, and had to be, his own master. He had nothing but contempt for men who sought to engage themselves to another.

Sussex still had a number of hiring, or statute, fairs. At Steyning Fair held on 12 October those wishing to take service ranged themselves in rows, men on one side of the road, women on the other, each bearing an appropriate badge of their calling.[2] Carters shouldered their whips, oxmen their goads, shepherds their crooks, sheep-shearers their shears, oddmen carried the implement with which they were most proficient. The young women, faces scrubbed, all smartly attired, smiled and curtseyed whenever a farmer and his wife loomed near. Potential employers scrutinised possible servants from head to heel, much as a dealer would a horse. Questions were put and answered on either side and, if the results were satisfactory, a contract for twelve months' service was made and a shilling paid as 'earnest money' to bind it.

No self-respecting traveller, Chewbacca least of all, would submit to such indignity. Even in winter, better to freeze under canvas on frost-hardened ground than wake under another's roof and be subject to their demands. And, in spring and summer, brother, there was no life possible except that of the roads.

Jemmy, their first child, was born to Chewbacca and Liddy in 1830. For the next ten years of their married life the couple returned after back-end fairs to winter in Ditchling. The Matthews family had long been connected with this Sussex village. Ann Matthews, a traveller, had brought her infant son, John, to be christened here in November 1755. It was probably this same John Matthews who returned to be buried in the local churchyard in January 1829. Chewbacca described himself as a pedlar whose normal abode was Ditchling when he took his second son to be christened John at Midhurst in May 1834.

In the early nineteenth century Ditchling had two attractions for travellers: good drinking water gushing forth in springs after filtering through Downland chalk, and an expanse of common. With Enclosure Acts encouraging landowners to gobble up commons and wastes, it was becoming more and more difficult to find atchin-tans anywhere.

On Ditchling Common and his other camping grounds Chewbacca could find the willow and junkers, or rushes, he needed for basketting. Even the short heathland rushes growing no more than a foot high were used to make children's round baskets but what, as a kipseydoeser, he most prized were tall bullrushes that could be woven with the least amount of joining. Then there were willows yielding their sallow-wands for sturdier baskets and all of nature's bounty to give colouring dyes – blue from dogwood berries, yellow from peat or heather, brown from brambles, green from nettles or privet berries, and bright red from ladies' bedstraw.

Ebernoe, Witley and Hindhead furnished for Chewbacca his most valuable materials: whitethorn, blackthorn and furze that he turned into walking sticks and umbrella handles. In this respect his depredations infuriated local people who had grazing rights or estovers on the commons. In order to bend the sticks into required shapes he steeped the furze in cauldrons over fires that too often laid wide areas to scorched waste.

Chewbacca, helped by his sons, also made wooden shovels, dolls, and dodgers – the name he used for small besoms for sweeping hearths – and these sold on his 'All a Penny' stall when he travelled to fairs. He and Liddy started out with few worldly possessions, but industry, cunning and thrift meant that Liddy's 'deep pocket' was never empty.

Before 1840 Liddy had given birth to two sons, Jemmy and John, the latter being christened at Midhurst on 25 May 1834, his father described as a pedlar from Ditchling. Phoebe appeared two years later, then in June 1839 Betsy was born at Walton-on-Thames, her father now described as a chair bottomer. All these chavvies had been born under the canvas of their rod-tent home, and, when they moved from fair to fair, Chewbacca carried their stuff on his back or led a donkey-barrow. There were, however, signs of a transport revolution destined to transform their lives.

Gypsies, impelled by the march of intellect, seemed resolved no longer to march afoot, and now travel the country in capacious machines larger than a Paddington omnibus, drawn by two or more horses. (*The Times*, 11 July 1833)

Showmen were among the first travellers to take advantage of improved roads and avail themselves of the new caravans. It was the proud boast of Liddy's third son that he was not born in a tent like a gypsy. William, later known as Redshirt Matthews, was christened in Godalming church in October 1843, at a time when Chewbacca had just built for his family a new home on wheels. Henceforth they would travel the fairs in style in their new horse-drawn house-cart.

Rod tent and horse-drawn wagons.

Chapter Two
TRAVELLING SHOWMAN

About sixteen couples followed, some half dozen or so – the nearest relatives – wearing black coats and the usual habiliments of mourning, the others all clean and tidily dressed, but in the varied gypsy garb.

(*Windsor & Eton Express*, 1 November 1862)

Chewbacca came from generations of travellers. He was born 17 June 1811 and on 23 June 1811 christened James at Chiddingly where the baptism entry names his parents as John and Jane Matthews, 'travellers of Ditchling'. Jane had previously given birth to three children – Elizabeth, christened at Uckfield in 1803, Jane at Brighton in 1806, and Joseph at Hailsham in 1809. Their heritage was not land, but the road that opened up in spring to lead them from one fair to the next and on; travelling the southern counties they wove the thread of its roads into a warp of fairs, clubs and feast days to create a web of seasonal magic.

Most of the fairs Chewbacca attended had been held since time immemorial. Findon and Weyhill fairs, sited close by prehistoric mounds and old, old trackways, betrayed their ancient origins. Others owed existence or formal recognition to medieval charters. Henry I granted Chichester's Sloe Fair to the Bishop, Henry II granted Bamet Fair to the Abbots of St Albans, and on a smaller scale in 1290 Ralph de Camvis granted people of Rogate the right to hold a fair annually.

In the early nineteenth century the chief purpose of most fairs was trade. People came together on special days of the year to buy and sell, to meet their friends and quite simply to enjoy themselves. But that religion rather than commerce inspired these occasions is clear from the names of old fairs and the fixed dates on which they were held. 'Fair' derives from *Feria*, a festival or holy day; in German the word for 'fair', *Messe*, also translates as holy mass. In some cases there is clear correlation between fairs and the dedication of the local parish church: in Sussex, Crawley and Wivelsfield held fairs on the feast days of St John the Baptist; there were fairs of the Holy Trinity at Cuckfield, St Laurence the Martyr at Hurstpierpoint, St Margaret at West Hoathly, St Martin at Westmeston and St Nicholas the Bishop at Portslade. Despite confusion caused by the calendar change in 1752 when eleven days were omitted in

September of that year, dates of other important fairs in the county show their connection with religious festivals. In Chichester, St George's Fair was henceforth held on 4 May instead of that saint's patronal day, 23 April, and St Denys's Fair was moved from 9 October to 20 October.

Fairs had been linked with church festivals as far back as A.D.601 when Pope Gregory wrote to St Augustine counselling him how best to treat the newly-converted English. Their pagan idols should be destroyed, of course, but not their temples, for these could be purified and consecrated to the service of the true God. And where local people had been accustomed to celebrate pagan festivals, so now they should be provided with other causes for celebration such as a day of dedication or the festival of the holy martyr whose relics had been enshrined in the church.

On such occasions they might well construct shelters of boughs for themselves around the churches that were once temples, and celebrate the solemnity with feasting. They are no longer to sacrifice beasts to the Devil, but they may kill them for food to the praise of God, and give thanks to the Giver of all gifts for His bounty. If the people are allowed some worldly pleasures in this way, they will more readily come to desire the joys of the Spirit.

(Bede's *History of the English Church and People*)

And so, worldly pleasures in the form of fairs became associated with saints' days. Local people having attended religious services in the morning spent the rest of the day in dancing, feasting and amusements.

Religion and pleasure formed the essence of these early festivals until, attracted by the crowds, came hawkers, pedlars, and eventually merchants to set up stalls and booths for the sale of their wares. At this stage the fairs developed an undeniably commercial aspect. By the 1840s the majority of large annual fairs were held ostensibly for the sale of animals, agricultural produce or specific types of merchandise.

There were sheep, cattle and horse fairs; cheese, hops and onion fairs; leather, wool and cloth fairs.

A new element in rustic festivities was introduced with the establishment of a multitude of village Benefit Societies in the first half of the nineteenth century. The Club Day jollities that took place on the occasion of the annual share-out were often timed to coincide with traditional local fair dates and incorporated some of the ritual of earlier festivals. For example, ceremonies attached to Harting Old Club originally took place on St John the Baptist Day. On Club Day folk, up since dawn, busied themselves selecting, cutting and peeling hazel wands. With these in their hands and dressed in white smocks the men marched widdershins around a beech bough 'tree' before solemnly processing into church.[1]

At Lancing, villagers enjoyed a festive meal and then hastened to the fair, the culminating point of their annual celebration.

Our little gathering called a 'fair' was beautiful! What a crowd of uncles, and aunts, and cousins, and neighbours, and young children, and old folks, and every body! And what a polite squeezable crowd it was to be sure! And what a spread of canvas! And what profusion of glittering riches under said canvas.

Come here my little dears, and fill out your little bags with gingerbread and oranges! Never mind the morrow. Blow the doctor! Fill your little bags once a year and be happy! Poor little souls! 'Tis but little you see of the magic of life, be happy while ye may. [2]

Billingshurst established its United Tradesmen's Friendly Society in 1832 and held its annual club day each June, but there was a furore the year a new vicar declined to preach the customary sermon after seeing posters advertising that the amusements would include dancing. Dancing, he alleged, had a strong tendency to debauchery and immorality. Club members found alternative benediction at the Independent Chapel whose minister, at an hour's notice, preached a sermon befitting the occasion. After this the proceedings passed off with great *éclat*, the vicar's anathema appearing to impart fresh vigour to dancing's devotees who tripped merrily through the night to the sound of the Arundel Brass Band.[3]

In addition to his 'All-a-Penny Stall', Chewbacca was trading with various forms of amusements consisting of Aunt Sallies and low stands on which he balanced snuff-boxes, tobacco-boxes, cheap trinkets, even half-pennies or gingerbread to be thrown at. Sometimes, too, he set up apples and oranges in small piles and in return for a half-penny invited punters to 'Knock down one, you have 'em all.' By the mid 1840s, although still described as a hawker of Ditchling, Chewbacca had moved his base

from Sussex into Surrey where the family settled for a few winters near Frensham Ponds. Their fourth son, Charles, was born in February 1846 and taken to Haslemere parish church to be christened.

In 1851 the Census officials caught up with Chewbacca, Liddy and their four youngest children back on the Sussex side of the border, living in a house cart at Iping Marsh. The following year, shortly before Christmas, Liddy bore her last child, Joseph, christened at Shottermill, near Haslemere, on 6 February 1853.

His proper christened name was Joseph, yer know, but everyone called him Harelip. More than often yer couldn't understand a word he spoke, nor yer couldn't, but it never seemed ter matter none. T'was just the way he were, yer see – and none of 'is fault. 'Cos the way it 'appened was this.

His dear mother was asittin' in her wagon one day jus' afore she had him. Sittin' up in her wagon doin' her lacework; quiet and on her own like. 'Cos the women they used to keep theyselves respectful in them days and wouldent be seed out if they was big wiv carryin'.

Wal, his dear mother now she was sittin' in her wagon never thinkin' of troubles, when in jumps this hare. Straight up, he did! This hare jumps right through the door in front of Liddy while she's expectin' and natchrally the chavvy when he were born has this crooked lip an' all.

It were the hare frittin' Liddy like that, yer see, what done it.

That was how Joseph's cleft palate came to be explained in the family. Everyone knew that expectant wives should avoid all possibility of contact with a hare, that they could not completely trust the efficacy of hare's-foot brooches to ward off malevolence. But poor Liddy, they realised, had been helpless once the hare had sought her out.

One of the events Liddy most looked forward to each year was Windsor's Onion Fair. It originated in a charter granted by Edward IV. It was usually proclaimed by the Town Mayor at twelve o'clock on 24 October and lasted two, sometimes three, days. Onions in fine strings, onions in baskets and sacks were on sale in the Market House under the Town Hall or on Castle Hill. The High Street thronged with shows, swings, toy and gingerbread stalls. The horse, cattle and pig fair took place nearby in Bachelor's Acre where, too, the owners of shooting-tents and knock-'em-downs set up their paraphernalia.

The Acre was always messy, often muddy, and when saturated by torrents of rain as it usually was at fair time it became a quagmire. This did not lessen its appeal for the Eton boys who, although strictly forbidden to attend the fair, year after year ran the gauntlet of College discipline to savour its delights.

One of Chewbacca's pals was a showman of strikingly diminutive stature called Joey Yelding. Joey had a set of knock-'em downs but made more money by operating a game of roulette, a strictly illegal form of gambling that proved irresistible to the Etonians. "Step up, step up, my little lords! Step this way," he'd shout. "And yer needn't fear the masters nabbing yer, 'cos we've got a look-out as will holler if anyone tries ter come arter yer." And so the game would proceed until rudely interrupted by the cry: "Master!" whereupon the boys fled wildly through the crowds.[4]

What Liddy loved about the fair was its proximity to the royal court and the chance that she would see the Queen come riding by. In 1847 Queen Victoria and Prince Albert, on leaving the castle for their afternoon's drive, proceeded into the High Street and then down Thames Street peering at the shows and booths as they passed.[5] The following day came a royal request for Wombwell's Menagerie to be shown in the Castle Quadrangle and for once Her Majesty *was* amused.

Wombwell's Menagerie at Windsor, 1847.

A glory of Windsor Fair was its gingerbread. Gingerbread thickly encrusted with 'gold' had been introduced into England from France in the reign of Henry IV, since which time no fair had been complete without stalls burdened with coppery gilded horses, birds, elephants, bishop's mitres, crosses and crowns. In 1848, year of revolutions, it was remarked that the gingerbread stalls 'exhibited gilded sovereignty and sold it as cheap as it has lately been reduced to on the Continent.' The fair was again honoured by a visit from the Queen and Prince Albert who drove through the bustling saturnalia of the High Street. The royal carriage made its appearance so suddenly out of Castle Street that it was not at first recognised, but as soon as its occupants were perceived they were greeted respectfully by the bystanders.

Her Majesty and the Prince seemed much to enjoy the motley and joyous though unpatrician festivity.
(*Windsor & Eton Express*, 28 October 1848)

Mama and Papa had seen and evidently approved. Before long younger members of their family were finding their way to the fair. In 1855 a royal party wandered along the High Street where a multitude of competing shows each boasted 'only correct views' of the battle of Alma, or Inkermann, or Balaklava – all three looking suspiciously alike. There were also several 'learned ponies' able to pick out from the crowd with uncanny accuracy 'the little boy who likes to dip his finger in the sugar basin' or 'the girl who likes to be kissed'.[6]

On the first morning of Windsor Fair in 1856 the Prince of Wales and Prince Alfred, chaperoned by their tutors, passed through the fair on horseback, plainly enjoying the mimicry of the showmen and the various grotesque scenes enacted. In the afternoon the Princess Royal, attended by a lady of the court, rode down Castle Hill and Thames Street in a carriage to see for herself what had excited her brothers.[7]

Earlier that year the Peace of Paris had formally ended the Crimean War. In July 1856 Queen Victoria, accompanied by the Prince Consort, the Prince of Wales and the King of the Belgians, travelled down to the newly-opened army camp at Aldershot to inspect the returning troops.

At Aldershot thousands of young men had been brought together with pay arrears in their pockets and good reason to seek diversion. The significance of this did not escape Chewbacca. He smartened up his equipment and with his family hastened down to Chobham Ridge. His son Redshirt, then a lad of thirteen, never forgot the scene they met there. He was asked in later life how it was that his family first began their long association with Aldershot.

My father came to that district because he saw business ahead in his line. The troops were returning from the Crimea, and our show proceeded to Chobham Ridge and took its share in providing entertainment for those poor chaps who had gone through months of hell. I can recall that Queen Victoria, with the Prince Consort, held a great review on the Ridges, and youngster though I was, I can still remember the sight.

You know that later on the camp was moved from Chobham to Aldershot. My father made Farnborough his headquarters but we were as much on the road as we were at home. Yes, there was plenty of money when the troops came home, and there was plenty to be made when the camp was being built. In our line there was plenty of business, for there was not much entertainment for the men, and the show and the fair were held in high favour. [8]

By the end of the fifties Chewbacca's eldest two sons had married and left the clan. Jemmy, wed to a travelling woman whose christian name was Famebridge, described himself as a chair-mender when their child was baptized in 1853. He had followed his father's footsteps into the prize ring, and during the horseracing season was often to be found in the crowded corners of the racecourse when a 'mill' was being arranged. At Brighton in 1869 he acted as second for James Skilton when he fought William Wilkins and killed him with his bare fists.

All three men were drinking in a booth on the Racehill when Wilkins, who travelled with swing-boats, asked Skilton to drink with him. Skilton declined, saying that if he wanted a drink he would pay for it himself. Then he took Wilkins's hat and was about to hit it.

"Sooner than you should hit my hat, I had rather you should hit me," cried Wilkins.

"Well, then we'll have a round or two," said Skilton. Their immediate intentions being frustrated by the police, they moved some distance up the race course, to about three hundred yards from the Grand Stand, and fought three or four rounds before both falling to the ground together. Wilkins fell underneath.

"You have hit me cowardly," were his last words.

Skilton was charged with manslaughter and Jemmy with aiding and abetting. In his dirty smock frock when arrested and worse for drink, Jemmy denied being present at the fight and the charges against him were dropped. [9]

Meanwhile, Chewbacca's eldest daughter, Phoebe, had married little Joe Yelding, but the couple were not among the great gathering of travellers at Hampton Wick for the annual pleasure fair held on Thames Bank or Barge Walk in 1861. Chewbacca and Lydia were there, recorded in the Census together with their twenty year old daughter, Mary Anne, and their youngest son, Joseph.

In September 1862, they travelled, as usual, to Barnet where, on the first weekend of the month, one of the country's biggest cattle fairs took place. Formerly as many as 45,000 animals were brought here each autumn to supply the London meat market, but with the introduction of root crops allowing stock to be fed over winter, the cattle trade declined. Barnet henceforth was known as a horse and pleasure fair. Before the construction of the railway line cut through the course the event also included horseracing.

Londoners by the thousand made a trip to Barnet Fair their annual treat, although it was readily acknowledged that it was not an occasion that appealed to high society.

Making a trip to Barnet Fair, 1914.

"One will look in vain for the Upper Ten Thousand, but there will be no difficulty in discovering the Lower Ten."[10]

No visitor was long at Barnet Fair before purchasing an ash stick to ward off too close an association with horses and clumsy hooves. Nor was it uncommon for petty squabbles suddenly to flare into violent assaults.

The horse-dealers were not renowned for fraternal feelings towards each other. Just let a potential customer look at a horse for some rival dealer immediately to warn him against buying it.

"He'd make a good soldier, guv'nor, that one. For I'm blest if I don't think he'd die afore he'd run."

From the top of Barnet Hill a bird's-eye view of the scene revealed on one side a long, long row of gingerbread stalls and booths for the sale of toys and glittering ornaments. Opposite was a row of shooting galleries with, for the most part, obtrusively importunate lasses in charge, and at the bottom ground was marked out for coconut shies.[11] Here one idle spectator calculated that for every nut he lost, the showman gained at least one shilling.[12]

At the end of September 1862 Chewbacca and Liddy moved on to Michaelmas Fair at Uxbridge, but the day was ruined by incessant rain. They probably stayed in the vicinity so that they could return to the town for its Old Michaelmas Fair on 10 October. Again heavy rain fell most of the day. Liddy felt unwell. She was sure she'd caught a chill – not surprising with such rotten weather.

And then it was time once again for Windsor's Onion Fair, but less eager anticipation for the event this year. Something of a pall seemed to lie over the town and there was no prospect of greeting the Queen as she made one of her sallies from the castle to drive through the shows. Since last Onion Fair tragedy had overtaken the royal family and the whole country. Prince Albert had been struck down in the prime of life by typhoid fever.

Townspeople in Windsor were doubly horrified by the death. They mourned the loss of a popular prince; they looked about themselves with dread as to the source of the contagion. The local newspaper was quick to dispel suggestions that sanitary arrangements in the borough were in any way defective. They maintained that Windsor was entirely free from gastric, typhoid, and any other form of fever, firmly rejecting allegations made in the *Examiner* that local people who died of typhoid were reckoned by their neighbours to have succumbed to 'the common Windsor fever'.[13] By the time of Onion Fair the period of public mourning was past, yet gloom still held over the town as Chewbacca's family

approached Windsor in October. Liddy had not recovered from her chill, was even a bit feverish and finding it difficult to breathe. Chewbacca pulled his wagon into North's Lane near the Acre, and sent for the doctor to come.

It was so hot in the wagon. "No air," moaned Liddy, and struggled to get off her bed before falling back, exhausted. She grew delirious and her mind wandered.

It was hot and so stuffy. She must get out, out into the open, into the fresh air. She had the baby, little Phoebe, cradled in her arm and was slithering over to the door of the tent. It was stuffy, she would get air. But it was dark, too. She fumbled clumsily trying to untie the opening. Before she managed to do so, she felt the weight on the canvas, pushed her free hand through a gap and clutched at impalpable all-encompassing snow.

She was trapped – trapped in a canvas tomb under goodness knows how many feet of snow. There were her chavvies to think about. They mustn't perish, not so young and all their lives before them. She would save them by burrowing a way out, up to the surface where they'd all be able to breathe cool refreshing air again. It was so hot, so close she must have … air. But, before she started, she knew it was hopeless. She wouldn't be able to tunnel upwards without filling the tent with snow in the process, and the tent would remain her refuge until it became her tomb.

It was so hot and clammy with the dense snow walls pressing in on her. She beat her arms in the air to hold back the walls of darkness. And then she remembered the chavvies, with mounting dread felt round in the bed for the baby that was not there, but now a woman grown. And young Jemmy and Johnny disappeared as if melted into and through the snow – leaving her trapped alone – but not alone now – because her man had come back for her, had heard her desperate cries and come for her.

"Jem-my, Jem-my," the name she had first known him by – moaned mechanically through her lips as she twisted her head from side to side at the height of the fever.

Never leaving her side, Chewbacca sat keeping her lips moistened with water. The doctor, when he arrived, made no effort to disguise his anxiety. Liddy was very sick, no doubt about that. He would see what he could do about having her admitted to the Infirmary.

Liddy moaned and began the hoarse whisper again: "Jem-my, Jem-my. Jem-my." They had not time to move her from the wagon. She died that evening, three days before the fair. As other travellers arrived in town they were devastated by the news.

There was the usual great attendance of showmen

at Onion Fair in 1862 and the usual huge crowds of people were expected. The High Street was closely packed with shows, stalls and swings. In the Acre the horse, cattle and pig fair took place as normal with space allocated to Dutch auctioneers, shooting galleries and knock-'em-downs. Undoubtedly the greatest attraction was Wombwell's Menagerie.

The announced feeding of the wild beasts and serpents in Wombwell's Menagerie did not attract so large a crowd as anticipated on Monday afternoon. Those present, however, appeared to be much interested at observing the special characteristics distinguishing the various animals, as far as supplying the demands of nature may be regarded. The elephant in whose capacious maw large loaves of bread rapidly disappeared was first fed. Then the spectators were amused at the awkward waddling of the pelicans in the direction of a pail of fish placed in the centre of the exhibition and at the rapid manner in which its contents were emptied.

The various species of the carnivore which included the lions, tigers, leopards, bears, etc. were then taken in succession. Their propensities were exhibited to advantage. Lastly, the sluggish serpents were fed with live young rabbits. These reptiles appeared scarcely to have arrived at that stage of hunger as to produce the usual voracity for food. At the same time some of them were tempted to seize the poor timid animals, which were then condemned to die by a process of slow torture which however curious formed a disagreeable spectacle. Although

on the whole the exhibition was not up to Wombwell's mark, the performance of the lions and leopards was worth witnessing.

A CONTRAST
While the fair and its amusements were at their height on Saturday, a scene of another kind (though brought to this locality by it) might have been witnessed at the Windsor cemetery - the burial of a gypsy wife named Matthews, aged 55, who died of bronchitis in her husband's van in North's Yard on the previous Tuesday. About sixteen couples followed, some half dozen or so – the nearest relatives wearing black coats and the usual habiliments of mourning, the others all clean and tidily dressed, but in the varied gypsy garb. Much interest was occasioned by the sad and unusual ceremony. Some of the funeral party attended the parish church on Sunday morning, and listened to the service with the greatest attention.[14]

It was the family's custom to go to church on the three Sundays following a death to say prayers 'to help the dear one on their way'. On this occasion Phoebe was not well enough to go with Chewbacca, his sons and younger daughter. Never strong, she had collapsed when she heard of her mother's death.

Amidst grief for the sudden death of Liddy, the family was frightened now for the health of her daughter. Their worst fear, however, they kept to themselves. The newspaper had clearly stated that Liddy died of bronchitis, but the registered cause of her death was – typhoid fever.

Liddy's death certificate.

Chapter Three
REDSHIRT AND POLLY

Billy Matthews was young then and, dressed in his red shirt, came as one of his father's assistants.
The roundabouts were not worked by steam in those days, but turned by a pony,
who walked, or ran round, inside the circle of the wooden horses.

J. Challacombe, *Jottings from a Farnborough Notebook* (1922)

Windsor's town mayor was adamant. Onion Fair was a two day Statute Fair which often continued into a third day. But not in 1862. The fair expired on Saturday night and would on no account be allowed any extension. What was more, said the mayor, all caravans and paraphernalia should be cleared away promptly. And so it was, as citizens went back to their shops and offices on Monday morning, some sad, some glad, that the annual junketings were over, life in the town quietly returned to normal.

Bachelor's Acre, emptied of gingerbread stalls, shows, shooting-galleries and other adjuncts of the fair, was silent and deserted except for a solitary wagon. Within lay Phoebe broken-hearted. From the day of her mother's death, she began to waste away. She had a husband and child, but neither could replace the mother to whom she had been bound so tightly, protected from harm and cold, in the shawl as a baby. At Barnet Fair three years later Phoebe Yelding died of tuberculosis. Obedient to her last wishes the family brought her body back to Windsor to lie with Liddy in the same grave.

The light was never rekindled in Chewbacca's life. In February 1872 Charles Godfrey Leland, eminent gypsiologist, called to see him. Conversation inevitably turned to the subject of the old man's sorrow. Leland was told: "It is nine years since my wife died, and I would give all Anglaterra to have her again."

The trouble was, in late October 1862 not only had Chewbacca none of Anglaterra to give, it was difficult for him to find even the smallest scrap of land to rest his home on. The town authorities naturally wanted to be quit of him and his family immediately, but where were they to go? There was Blackwater Fair coming up, and Farnham's November Fair he had always attended – but that was when Liddy had been alive. Now it was different. For the first time in his life, Chewbacca had no urge to be on the road.

To take to the road was to leave Liddy behind. Besides, many travellers were aware of the fever and were trashed; some of them treating Chewbacca's family as if they were all mochardi. It was understandable. They worried, not so much for themselves, but for the affect on flatties the fear of contagion might have. Once townspeople got the idea that travellers were bringing typhoid into their midst, the fairs would be killed instantly.

Chewbacca could only lie low until the panic and rumours subsided; he did not contradict anyone who said that Liddy died of bronchitis. Harelip, her youngest chavvy, was barely ten years old but the rest of the family had all reached an age to be independent.

Fortunately, Mary Ann was still unwed and able to look after her father's wagon and manage daily chores. That situation, however, did not last long. For some time she had been courted by Henry Bailey, travelling photographer, whom she married at Aldershot in June 1863. During the summer months Chewbacca often travelled in their company.

A few years after Liddy's death he joined them for a trip from Haslemere to Epsom, combining business with the pleasure of meeting up with old pals at the Races. The weather was warm and the little party stopped for refreshment many times en route – growing happier with each mile. At Guildford on Saturday evening all three – Chewbacca, Mary Ann and Henry Bailey – were charged with being drunk and disorderly. The men admitted they were drunk and were fined ten shillings each, but they didn't have to put their own hands in their pockets to find the money. Mr Superintendent Law had already searched them and had confiscated, he said, more than sufficient money to pay the fines. What was more, he had discovered in the course of his search that Bailey had on him a partridge's egg which the police officer now proudly produced in court as substance for another charge.

"I have a child ill with measles and I had the egg given me by Bill Luff, the carrier of Haslemere," Bailey pleaded before being discharged pending further enquiries.[1]

In his declining years Chewbacca came to rely on his third son, Redshirt, for support. Redshirt was nickname for the child christened William in Godalming in 1843. Almost eighty years later, nearing the end of his own long life, Redshirt reminisced:

I was born at Shackleford, Godalming, in a caravan. I am the son of James Matthews, a Sussex showman ... Like all showmen's children I, of course, came into the concern. We had in those days more of a bazaar than a show. I mean my father's business eighty years ago was not to be regarded as my own show today, but there were plenty of side attractions, and as a boy I remember that wherever we went there pleasure and entertainment always followed. [2]

At West Molesey in the parish church on the day of the summer solstice, 1861, Redshirt had married Mary Ann, daughter of Bennie and Annie Bushnell, knife-grinders. Polly, as she was always called, had been born on the road to another family that had travelled for generations – which was all the dowry she needed to marry a Matthews.

The newly-weds spent their honeymoon on the road between Molesey and Farnham on their way to Midsummer Fair. Farnham was the venue of three annual fairs attended by Redshirt. The first held originally on Ascension Day, but later fixed for 10 May; Midsummer Fair on St John's Day; the third in November, formerly on the thirteenth but later changed to the tenth.

The regular arrival of travellers into a quiet country town like Farnham was in itself a momentous event. Fair day was a holiday for all the school children. Their excitement mounted as the wagon-people who had been waiting for hours in nearby lanes came pouring into town on the previous evening precisely on the stroke of six by the church bell. The showmen immediately set to staking out their pitches in Castle Street.

Soon after dawn the following morning the hullabaloo started. Down the street charged a herd of black Welsh bullocks brought over from Blackwater Fair; then an aimless flock of sheep wandering from side to side with dogs yapping in frenzy at their heels. A showman, held up by a broken wheel back on the road, arrived to find his usual pitch taken and made loud protest. At public house doors dishevelled gypsies were quarrelling off deals. Well-dressed farmers gathered in groups and then were forced to leap aside as a horse-coper ran a frightened horse through the crowd to show its paces.

Setting up the coconut shy. These 'coconut trees' were abandoned because they made it easier to knock the nuts out and too many were smashed in the process.

Folk yelled, horses clattered, sheep bleated – and school children tried to compete by blowing into their toy trumpets just purchased at one of the stalls. Guns popped at shooting-galleries. "Ev'ry one a good 'un", screamed a showman, while his neighbour hammered in stakes as he finished building up his stall.[3]

In Castle Street were stalls selling edible fairings – gingerbread, of course, and Garibaldi biscuits, sugar-sticks, hundreds-and-thousands, hard-bake. Others proffered pots and pans, crockery-ware, china dogs, and wooden toys. And where were Redshirt and Polly in all this noisy chaos? Further up Castle Street Polly was standing in front of her tube-shooter.

Redshirt had been quick to exploit the fact that target shooting had recently become a popular pastime. He had constructed a tube about twenty feet in length with a target at one end enclosed in a bullet-box with a steel back plate. In this way patrons could fire rifles even in crowded streets with relative safety. The target was illuminated by a naphtha flare lamp and, if the marksman's bullet passed through the bull's-eye hole in the centre it would send a striker swinging against a bell. At Farnham Fair Polly looked after the shooting-gallery. Redshirt managed their coconut shy and knock-'em-downs, but his eye was on the swing-boats and horse-drawn roundabouts owned by more prosperous showmen.

Streets the day after were littered by piles of hurdles, general filth and clutter – one reason why the newly formed Local Board came to loathe the fairs. In June 1867 they complained to the Town Hall Company, owners of the fair site, about the mess left after the recent fair in Castle Street. This proved but the opening salvo in a battle to rid Farnham of what the Board deemed 'the Fairs nuisance', but even after the Fairs Act of 1871 there was little they could do, because the fairs were held on private land.

After his marriage Redshirt saved up enough money to buy a set of swing-boats. Polly continued to mind the shooting gallery but her hands were also full with looking after chavvies. Their first child, a girl christened Phoebe, was born in 1864. Then came Anne and Lydia. Their fourth daughter, Lavinia, died of dropsy at Cuckfield in 1872 when the family were making their sad way back from Lindfield Fair. Within the next ten years Polly gave birth to two more daughters and five sons.

The couple must have been hard put to earn enough to feed their growing family. On one occasion Redshirt set out alone to walk from Farnborough to Houndsditch to buy some cheap swag. He carried his money in a nosebag slung over his shoulder. Before reaching his destination he was set upon by thieves who, after a bloody battle, made off with all his cash, leaving him to return scarred and dispirited to Polly.

Redshirt also made money from horse dealing and in slack periods used his carts to transport gravel for the Camp. Polly sometimes hawked baskets and wooden flowers at winter fairs, especially just before Christmas. It was while she was doing this one year that a gentleman she had met in the past came up to renew acquaintance.

In the 1870s travelling people were much sought after by ardent scholars anxious to pick up any crumb of their hidden language and lore. This was the age of the Romany Rye; Charles Godfrey Leland and Francis Hindes Groome were chief exponents of the cult. In December 1873 the two gentlemen set out together for Cobham Fair to indulge in a little 'gypsying'.

'At Cobham Sam Smith appeared, looking very neat – also Bowers and other diddikais. Sam invited us to drink – and I then invited them all. As we all spoke Romany pretty freely, the result was that the two or more policemen eyed Mr Groome and myself very earnestly and appeared to be looking after us during the day. . .' Leland's innocent delight at being kept under the eye of the law was increased when he spotted yet another traveller he knew. He probably remembered Polly from eighteen months previously when he had called on her father-in-law, and now, in front of the younger man, he was able to take advantage of that earlier meeting.

'We walked along the road and met a Gypsy woman who knew me, Mrs Matthews, peddling. She was much nicer than most of them. She thought that Groome must be my son. We asked her to come to an ale-house and drink, but she demurred to being a cause of disgrace to two such gentlemen. So I told her to follow us in, and we went into a queer little old tavern… Another Gypsy woman was seen approaching. We opened the door and Mrs Matthews in great glee called her in, as did I and Mr Groome, all speaking Romany. I never saw astonishment so vividly portrayed on a human face. As she slowly entered she stared at me and at her friend – as if in a dream. There was Mrs Matthews – *en famille* with two gentlemen – in gloves with lorgnons – but they were talking fluently – especially the younger – in the language of the roads.

'Then there came yet another named Lee – a black-eyed, hawk-nosed, fierce, and rather handsome young woman – and she was even more dumbfounded, and went and wedged herself in the extreme corner, and was almost afraid to drink her ale …

'Mr Groome was very lively, talking Romany so fluently that we all burst out laughing again and again. Mrs Matthews conversed with more intelligence than is usual among Gipsies. Once she said, "As if we weren't all alike to God – doesn't his sun shine the same on a Romany as on my Lord Duke?"

'She apologised for not standing treat in turn. So after much fun we broke up the party.'[4]

It would have been quite out of character for Polly to stand treats for fine gentlemen. Both she and Redshirt were careful with money, saving it to invest in more sophisticated fairground equipment. First Redshirt bought better swing-boats. Eventually he had two hundred pounds saved up, enough to purchase a roundabout. This was before steam had been brought to bear on them, and so he acquired a two-abreast twenty-four horse 'Dobby' set, measuring thirty-four feet in diameter. It was turned by a pony who walked or ran round inside the circle of wooden horses, and the ride quickly became a favourite with local children when it appeared at Farnborough's Club Day.

Redshirt's brother-in-law, little Joe Yelding, continued to travel with the Matthews family after the death of his wife Phoebe. He was remembered at Farnborough as a character, standing on a high stool behind his roulette table, shouting out his time-honoured call for customers:

Dobby-set at Wickham Fair c.1900. The pony pulling it round is just visible.

Even betting on the black,
Two to one on the red
Five to one on the blue,
Eight to one on the yellow,
A shilling on the crown and feather
Back 'em up, gentlemen, Back 'em up;
Play for pence, shillings or pounds.[5]

There were so few forms of organised entertainment in the countryside in those days, scarce wonder that festivals, clubs and feast days were celebrated with gusto, and the showmen who brought the latest amusements into their midst were welcomed by local people with something like awe – or, occasionally, disgust. At Windsor Onion Fair in 1863 the novelty at one show was a Kaffir eating live rats, until the Mayor ordered it to be stopped.[6] Two years later a 'talking fish' excited much wonder.[7] Then came the sight, sound and speed of the first steam roundabouts, and their attraction did not pall despite the difficulties some riders had in keeping their mounts. In 1867 it was reported from Windsor Fair that 'a girl fell from a horse on the steam Merry-go-Round when it was moving at great velocity and suffered a severe scalp wound.'[8] As soon as Redshirt saw one of the new steam roundabouts, he lusted after it. Expensive, well beyond the reach of a struggling family man, but he wanted one of these machines and, he resolved, the day would come ... Meanwhile, with more humble amusements he began to establish a reputation in a wide locality.

'He was a kind and generous man, and loved children, and for their sakes made no charge for his attendance at the school treats. He generally came himself, wearing his red shirt, and had a pleasant word for everybody', recalled Jessie Challacombe in *Jottings from a Farnborough Notebook*. But these school treats, village clubs and one-off celebrations were gaffs to be fitted in between the great traditional fairs that dominated a travelling showman's calendar.

The first fair of the year in Surrey was the Winter Fair held at Godalming on 13 and 14 February. While representatives of the hoop and timber trade consorted in the chief hotels of the town, the fair up until the early 1880s was held in the Brighton Road. One gloomy weather prophecy attached to it ran: 'If the sun shines before twelve o'clock on Godalming Fair Day the winter is not half over.'

Later, as Easter approached, Redshirt got his tackle ready for the road in earnest. There was so much to think about. Wagons to repaint, wheels to check, axles to grease, dobbies, swings and sideshows to pack, and dozens of horses and their fodder to be organised. And, then, the little gaffs to be foraged like wild flowers along the wayside as the outfit journeyed between annual fairs.

Redshirt had certain idiosyncrasies when it came to booking ground. His daughter Amy thus described her father's way of doing business.

'He couldn't read nor write any, but he managed everything himself – and there wasn't the man who derred cross him in any way, 'cos he was handy with his fists, yer know, when he needed to be. No, he couldn't read nor write but he took care of all the bookings and suchlike for the family. And the way he'd do it was this.

'He'd ride out in his pony and cart on his own and go on into villages and towns where he wanted to open. Then he'd put in tenders for grounds and when they was accepted, he would place his cross on the contract.

'So, at the end of the day he comes back to the family and says – not a blinkin word. And it don't matter if we says: "Well, come on tell us, Father, where we goin' arter Petworth?" "Never you mind, my dears, I've fixed it," he'd say, and there was no tapping him.

'No, he'd never tell anyone where he was going next, but kept all his bookings and dates safe in his head, and then, once we'd pulled down and were ready to move, orf he went in his pony and cart again at the head of the procession into the road. And he'd lead the way leaving signs on the road for us others to follow. Sometimes he'd have a sack of hay at his side, yer see, and he'd scatter a handful every time he turned a corner. And other times he'd take a bag of

Redshirt taking his favourite drink.

confetti and leave a little mound of that when he changed direction.

'And then, when me father arrived at the ground, he'd wait till his big wooden chair was brought out for him to sit in so's he could supervise building-up. Every ride or stall had to be situated 'xactly where he said, and whiles he was giving out his orders one of us girls would take him his favourite drink. And you know whatever that was? A raw egg beaten up in tea – and he used to drink that from his big round willow-pattern cup an' saucer.

'Yes, I can still see 'im sitting in that chair, giving out his orders, as clear nor it was yesterday. And wearing his red shirt, allus wore a red shirt, never knew him in nothing else, and that's what give him his name: Redshirt Matthews. Although, there agen, the chavvies used to call him 'Brandy Ball Bill', 'cos he loved chavvies, and allus carried a bag of them sweets in his pocket to give to them.

'Not that he were soft, mind. He wasn't very tall, but big built and strong with it. Yer know, he wasn't a man you'd cross.'

The family were regular visitors to Petworth because, like Farnham, it hosted three annual fairs. After the May Cattle Fair held traditionally on the first of the month, there were further cattle fairs in September and November. Petworth Winter Fair on 20 November was particularly important for Redshirt, but no matter how good the takings were, his family always groaned when the fair day neared its end. In front of them lay an almighty scramble to pull down, travel over twenty miles and then immediately build up again in time to open at Guildford Fair on 22 November.

For many showmen this was their last big gaff of the season, one at which rivalry for pitches often frayed tempers already strained by fatigue. In 1875 North Street was the scene of a pitched battle between the rival clans of Matthews and Ayres, ending with a number of broken noses, black eyes and summonses for assault.[9] Joe Yelding together with Chris Odam,

husband of Polly's sister, were charged in 1881 with obstructing Woodbridge Road by placing their wagons on the roadside waste on the night of 21 November whilst waiting to come into Guildford Fair. Each was fined five shillings and cautioned, the police making it clear that this should be a warning for the future.[10]

Stock was short in the cattle fair that year, and in the evening the pleasure fair, now limited to one day's duration, was also disappointing. Edward Ayres and Sam Smith who were attending with coconut shies drowned their sorrows in a local inn, exchanged customary insults, and then finished the day in style. The clans gathered on wasteland near Woodbridge Road to watch them strip to the waist for action. However, the pugilistic pair were arrested before they reached a conclusion.[11] Two other fairs were held annually at Guildford in the nineteenth century. May Fair, on the fourth of the month to give showmen a chance to come on from Petworth, was primarily for the sale of sheep and cattle, the sheep being penned in the fair field and the cattle exhibited in North Street. In 1874 the pleasure fair was larger than usual with well over fifty show carts blocking up Woodbridge Road the day before, ready to disgorge their contents. These included a long array of roundabouts, rifle galleries, Cheap Jacks, sparring booths, fat women and skeleton men – shows all open to the public at a penny a time.[12]

Then in early October there was Cat-on-Hill Fair where youths assembled in force to pelt each other with chestnuts.

Redshirt's travelling year having possibly started as early as February in Godalming, or March in Odiham and taken in visits to Horsham, Petworth, Farnham, Guildford, Knaphill, Ewell, Mitcham, Barnet, Windsor and Old Deer Park, Richmond, for public holidays, landed him back on his own doorstep after back-end. There was Hartley Wintney on 4 December and Farnborough Cattle Fair the following day.

In 1882, Farnham's Midsummer Fair was larger than usual with stalls and booths on both sides of Castle Street occupying so much space, and the crowd being so great, it was difficult to get the cattle through at all late in the day. This did not matter too much, because the stock trade was very dull and the attendance of farmers and dealers small.[13] The atmosphere of the crowded street was captured in a photograph showing Redshirt's coconut sheet with its legend:

W. MATTHEWS BOWLING
SALOON
1d a ball - 1 ball 1 nut
7 for 6d - all coconuts warranted
School treats attended

Matthews family at Castle Street Fair, Farnham, early 1880s.

Behind can be seen the centre pole and swifts of a roundabout and in the foreground a tall striker crowned with the Prince of Wales's feathers. Standing to the left is a short, stout figure, wearing a smock and with a felt hat shading his battered face. He looks as if he has been through the mill, and he had. Chewbacca Matthews, former prize-fighter, had participated in many a good 'mill' in his time, but his shadowy presence here at Castle Street in the early 1880s is living reminder of a past already fading fast.

In July 1883 Joey Yelding set out to ply his trade at Aldershot Races. During the course of the day he drank heavily. On his return home he fell between the shafts of his wagon and broke his neck.[14] He was buried in Cove cemetery. When Chewbacca died a few years later, aged seventy-nine, he was buried

there, too. Just as mother and daughter rested together in Windsor, now their respective menfolk lay side by side at Cove.

Chewbacca's grave at Cove. It bears a text from Psalm 90: *So teach us to number our days, that we may apply our hearts unto wisdom.*

Chapter Four
GENIAL TYRANT

He rules his little kingdom with a firm but kindly hand. He is up with the break of dawn
and personally attends to the many and varied duties of a showman's life.
To talk with him is like taking a dip into the pages of Hogarth.

(*World's Fair*, 25 September 1920)

The Camp at Aldershot had continued to grow apace. In the summer there were days when the sandy, unmade roads swirled into dust clouds as the carts trundled by. In winter more often than not the wet tracks churned into chrome-coloured mud as the same unending stream of carts arrived with yet more building materials. Each year after the back-end fairs, Redshirt and fellow travellers supplemented their fairground takings by driving carts carrying gravel to wherever it was needed.

At the time of the 1881 Census there had been several clans of travellers resident in or near North Camp. Living in tents in Yeovil Road were the families of Alfred Bowers, Sam Smith, and Paul Ayres. Nearby were the caravans of Redshirt Matthews and Joe Yelding, parked in Gravel Road on the spot today officially designated 'Mathews Close'.

A frequent sight on the roads was the little huddled figure of Prissy Bowers, in close fitting bonnet and Welsh shawl, leading her donkey cart.

"Guvverment remishun I 'as, ter do this," she declared proudly, and on occasion would produce her magic piece of paper permitting the bearer to pass between the lines for the purpose of supplying the troops with fruit and sherbet.

Prissy, born at Coombe, near Kingston-on-Thames, in May 1829, daughter of Joseph and Priscilla Dean, had a fighting reputation among travellers which would not have shamed Borrow's Isopel Berners. At Knaphill Fair in 1869 a fellow showman hit her son. Prissy grabbed a stick, waded in and beset all about her.[1] The Camp was no genteel place, but it would have been a doughty soldier who ventured to take liberties with this little woman as she plied her trade

 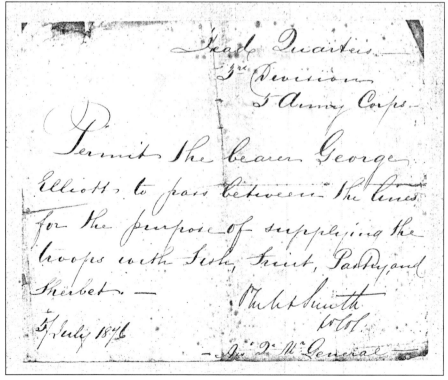

Above left: Prissy Bowers, a fizzer-seller at Aldershot Camp.   *Above right*: A permit like this enabled Prissy to ply her trade.

Redshirt Matthews's family.

of 'fizzer-seller'. Prissy Bowers, alias Smith, alias Dean, was mother of Andrew Smith and One-eyed Betsy, both of whom would interweave their destinies with the Matthews clan in later years.

1883 was a year of decision for Redshirt.

Polly had just given birth to their tenth surviving, and what was to prove their last, child – a girl christened Amy. His eldest daughter, Phoebe, was nearly eighteen, able really to pull her weight in the family. And then there were the five boys – Billy, a sturdy eight-year old and already working alongside his father like a man, James, Joe, Micky, and Johnny still a babbie. Five sons, there was nothing a man couldn't and shouldn't achieve backed by five strong sons. Redshirt counted his sovereigns and went off to see Frederick Savage of King's Lynn, manufacturer of machines and Merry-go-rounds. The firm's Engine Register recorded the following order:

DATE:	1883
NO:	282
DESCRIPTION:	Make 1 No. 2 vertical organ engine
SOLD TO:	W. Matthews
OTHER DETAILS:	....

DATE:	1883
NO:	285
DESCRIPTION:	Make 1 double cylinder
SOLD TO:	W. Matthews
OTHER DETAILS:	For 2-abreast 24-horse 'Dobby' set; 34′ diameter with truck and gear.

Redshirt Matthews was about to take society not by storm, but by steam!

When he first travelled his steam-driven horses, Redshirt was still dependent on the live animals for transport. It was five years before he followed up his order at Savages with another for 'one 6 h.p. traction engine, 8 ins. bore x 10 ins. stroke; fitted with steel relieving gear'.

Before this he kept more than a hundred horses. On the road four horses were used to pull the centre truck; there would be three horses on each of the big loads and two on the wagons. When in Farnborough, most of the horses were kept in a field in Park Road, although Redshirt also built stabling for thirty in Gravel Road.

His youngest son, John, known always as Chicken, early on revealed natural skill with animals, especially dogs and horses. Once a sick American colt was brought to him with a lump on the side of its head.

"I know what this is and I think I can deal with it," said young Chicken. "It's strangles."

He fetched a bucket containing linseed oil mixture, dipped some sacking in the concoction and tied it round the horse's head. The lump came up and up. Chicken plunged his penknife in boiling water and cut the swelling across the middle. Then he pressed out the poisonous matter and bathed the swelling repeatedly until the colt was cured.

In common with most travellers, from time to time Redshirt was accused of 'poovin his grais' in private fields. In Aldershot, near Manor Park, the authorities erected a pound for animals turned out to graze on War Department land. The exorbitant charges made for redeeming an animal often led to violent scenes when travellers under cover of night tried to release their horses without paying.

In January 1886 Redshirt was summoned for allowing seven horses to stray on the public highway at Ash. He patiently explained that they must have broken out of the meadow where he had left them. The Bench fined him £1.[2] On another occasion his horses got into a farmer's field near Liphook where they amused themselves by eating and rolling in about an

Redshirt's steam gallopers at Basingstoke with members of his family and Chaps. Among those sitting on the platform are 'Chicken' Matthews in striped jersey, and Richard and John Wall, the two young boys.

acre of oats, causing over fifteen pounds worth of damage. Redshirt was fined two guineas after protesting that only two of the miscreants were his.

One of the first gaffs visited by Redshirt's steam-driven roundabout was Petworth Winter Fair. In 1883 this event was threatened with abolition. As a result of a memorial signed by four hundred of the town's inhabitants it was reprieved and, despite the continued decline of the stock fair on Hamper's Common, the pleasure fair gained in popularity.[3]

In 1886 Matthews's Merry-go-round was the main attraction, especially with the young folk. From the time of starting until closing the horses' backs were scarcely empty.[4]

Then came the year of the Queen's Golden Jubilee and it seemed as if everyone locally wanted to secure Redshirt's steam roundabout as part of their festivities. In the first week of July 1887 he opened at Ash in Mr Hall's meadow where they were holding their jubilee fête, before moving back to Farnborough for their celebrations. After that he pulled into Aldershot Lodge Park for a grand fête on 20 July.[5] The weather for the occasion was splendid, even a trifle too hot for the children dressed up to take part in the mid-day procession. More than a dozen marquees and refreshment tents had been laid out with tea tables nicely decorated with flowers. On one

side of a large tent, printed in white letters on a red ground, was the motto:

VICTORIA, HEAVEN BLESS YOU & PROSPER YOUR AFFAIRS & SEND US PEACE

On the opposite side appeared:
*LOVE ALL, TRUST A FEW,
DO WRONG TO NONE*

For the Victorians, it seemed, when dealing with your fellow men, canniness was next to Godliness. Redshirt approved this caution. When asked in later years how he had come by all his money, he thought hard before replying.

"I'm going to give you a straight answer," he then said, "I got it by hook AND by crook."

On 30 June 1888 a letter appeared in the *Surrey & Hants News*:

*To the Editor
Sir – I have no doubt that a great many rate-payers know that the owners of the different stalls, shows, bowling-alleys, etc. pay a toll for standing room, but they are at a loss to know why the Farnham Town Hall Company collects and appropriates the toll. This amounts to a large sum for the three fairs held during*

the year. The day following you will find the Urban Sanitary Authority send their men, and cart, to sweep and clear the rubbish. You see that the Town Hall Company benefits by the fairs, but the Farnham Ratepayers are the losers. I hope some independent member of our Urban Authority will think this over before the next monthly meeting.

Ratepayer.

The Local Board needed no such reminder of their pet aversion: the Fairs in general, and Redshirt Matthews in particular.[6] Many Farnham residents had not greeted his steam roundabout with the enthusiasm bestowed on it elsewhere. They objected to its noise, to its smoke, and to its owner. The Board communicated its disapproval of Mr Matthews to the Town Hall Company. The Company served Redshirt notice that they would not allow him to build up his roundabout on their ground at the November fair. He ignored their notice. The Board decided to take a stand. Down to the fair marched their Surveyor and their Clerk. Together they warned Redshirt against playing the roundabout's organ. He ignored them.

At their next meeting when the problem of the fair was raised the Board rather meekly decided that it was a matter best left to individual inhabitants of the town. The challenge was taken up by a local doctor who secured an injunction to prevent Redshirt using the organ during the Midsummer Fair the following year. In the witness box, Dr Lorimer stated that the organ in question was played on fair days from early in the afternoon until nearly midnight; it was impossible to do any work of an intellectual nature in the houses near it; in fact it nearly drove the inhabitants mad.

It was all a point of view. Petworth with the same phenomenon erupting regularly in its midst kept consensus in favour of their pleasure fair with all its clamour and disturbance. Naturally, there were protesters against Redshirt's organ blaring forth from eleven in the morning to eleven at night, but many more attested that they actually enjoyed the sound.

The *West Sussex Gazette*'s reporter was evidently a fan of the fair, if his report of 26 November 1891 is anything to go by.

Petworth was very busy on Friday last on the occasion of the annual Winter Fair, which, after the lapse of so many years, and in spite of the attacks made on it, still survives to give a little freedom and a little amusement to a host of people, who come into the town from all the adjacent villages, even from distant Loxwood and Plaistow. The fixture was rendered more popular this year perhaps on account of its happening on the same date as Lord Leconfield's cottage audit, which brings several

hundred visitors to Petworth in the way of cottagers. A more comfortable looking lot of folk than these it would certainly be difficult to find, a fact chiefly due to large gardens, low rents, and the inherent industry of the labouring classes in our district.

The morning was taken up with business on Hamper's Common, where the attendance and stock, we regret to say, was much under the average.

If business was dull, the pleasure seekers were busy enough in the Market Square which, as usual, was completely filled with caravans of every sort and condition.

To Matthews' hippodrome (or in more prosaic language 'roundabouts') must be given the first place, and Mr Matthews seemed to wield the sceptre of an autocrat. He it was who gave the signal to commence business and who virtually wound up the concern soon after midnight. The visitors never seemed to tire of hearing the exquisite mixture on the organ of 'Hi tiddle hi ti!' and 'Love's old sweet song,' interspersed with the shrill screams of the handsome little engine 'that did all the work'.

With the gradual decay of stock and hiring fairs many people felt that annual pleasure fairs had lost their justification, but there were few who refused to welcome 'all the fun of the fair' at times of national celebration. The Diamond Jubilee was an opportunity for Redshirt to prove his social worth (and to make a tidy profit). At Farnborough's jamboree one youngster complained that rides on Mr Matthews' roundabout were not one of the free gifts of the show. Looking at the crowded ride, it was felt that would have been too tall an order.

At the time of the Jubilee the newly-invented cinematograph was evolving through the hands of Randall Williams and George Biddall into the travelling Bioscope shows which soon became popular features at country fairs. Royal spectacles, even sad ones, provided opportunities for these showmen.

Midsummer Fair at Farnham in 1901 included a cinematograph exhibition at the top of Castle Street. Crowds flocked in the evening to see pictures of the Queen's funeral. But there was another novelty in Crown Meadow. Besides his steam-driven horses blaring forth their music, Redshirt had acquired a new roundabout in the form of the 'Newmarket Racers' or patent bicycles. For the modest copper people were able to enjoy the privilege of pedalling in a linked circuit. Although not many indulged in three or four rides in succession, it was well patronised. And it was quieter.[7]

Some compromise had been reached. The roundabouts were now built up in the meadow, leaving the stalls, coconut shies and shooting-galleries in Castle Street, but there was still room for grievance. At the November Fair in 1902 a shooting gallery came under verbal fire when the window of Mr Bodkin's tailoring establishment proved the target for one marksman, whilst another leaden missile penetrated the bedroom overhead.[8]

Open shooting galleries had begun to replace the old-fashioned 'Tubes'. The new ranges, with their choice of static or moving targets, held the attention of the crowds more; the marksman taking aim at a bottle, or at a ball dancing on a jet of water, being exposed to the scrutiny and criticism of spectators. His misses were no longer veiled (or his triumphs darkened) within the recesses of the tube.

Amy, Redshirt's youngest daughter, knew just how to exploit military vanity when the fair was open at Aldershot.

'It was my job to look after the shooting gallery, and 'course I used to flirt a bit with the young soldiers, didn't I? And theys couldn't resist a challenge from a gal now, could they? "Wager yer a shillun on the first bull's eye, gentlemen," I'd say. Well, they puts down their shilluns an' takes oh! such careful aim. Where's me, I jus' picks up the gun and fires it anyhow-like. Most o' the time I don't even put a bloomin' bullet in me gun – but I allus wins the shillun! 'Course, what I never lets 'em see is the bit o' string I've tied to the heel of me shoe to jerk the bell to mark a bull's eye arter I've fired. Yes. Allus won me shillun, I did."

Tragically, where there were guns there was possibility of accidents. Amy's sister, Lydia, had married fellow-showman, Harry Verney. In July 1905 Amy was helping them in their shooter at Headley Fair. They were very busy. While the two young women were taking the money, Harry ducked back and forth putting the bottle targets up again. Somehow a gun went off aimlessly and Harry was killed. There was no social security to help his young widow and her chavvies. Naturally, they leaned back on Redshirt for support. Fortunately he was in a position to supply their material needs.

Redshirt at sixty-two years of age was still at the peak of his powers, covering hundreds of miles of roads through the summer months, especially now that he did not have to rely on horses to pull heavy loads. With the big steam haulers they were able to clear overnight and provide all the fun of the fair a matter of thirty or more miles away by the following day. As he explained:

"In clearing and fitting everybody knows his part - and does it. That is one of the secrets of our success. In the old days perhaps we needed a week to travel with our wagons and loads, but today the stuff can get on ahead and leave the living-wagons to take their leisure.

"It's a splendid life. In fact, you love it till you die. I mean it seriously. It is a life that has its ups and downs, and I've had both, but you are healthy and fit, and you don't get half the troubles nor ailments of the flattie.

"Take the spring morning on the edge of a leafy copse or common when we are on the road. You turn into the wagon at the close of day and you are up with the singing of the lark. It doesn't take long for the kettle to boil, and if you would ever enjoy a bit of frizzled bacon, why, just travel along with me for a few weeks, a better holiday you'll never have spent."

People were intrigued by Redshirt, by his odd mixture of toughness and vulnerability, self-effacement and pride. Always dignified, he possessed the sort of practical wisdom that attracted all manner of men to seek out his company. People who had seen his little collection of amusements expanding with the years, greeted the returning travellers annually with: "I wonder what Mr Matthews will be bringing with him this time?"

Of course, showman that he was, Redshirt's outfit was designed to attract attention. He also jealously safeguarded his pitches.

His eldest daughter, Phoebe, married Dicky Wall, a young man who had the temerity to order a set of gallopers from Savages almost identical to the set already owned by his father-in-law. Redshirt first saw Wall's roundabout built up at Drayton Manor. He stood silently, taking in the heads of kings and queens on the rounding boards, the gleaming paint work, everything spanking new.

He turned abruptly on his heel and made for his wagon, returning with a horsewhip to drive the competitor from his territory.

Steam gallopers purchased new by Dicky Wall.

Chapter Five
ROYALTY ON HIS ROUNDABOUTS

The Prince then paid a visit to the Chapel and later on in the day passed through the Country Fair, and insisted on taking a very senior officer of the College on to the merry-go-round.
(*Royal Military College Magazine*, Michaelmas Term,1921)

Prince Albert had first promoted the idea of building a home for the British army at Aldershot, and successive sovereigns continued to take an interest in its development. Royal involvement in the Camp manifested in many brilliant reviews and other ceremonies staged in Aldershot, which came to rival London and Windsor in the number of visits it received from the British royal family and foreign heads of state.

Prince of Wales on Redshirt's Roundabout, 1921.

In 1893 the Queen's son Arthur, Duke of Connaught, was appointed General Officer Commanding and moved into Government House. Under his command twenty-seven thousand troops paraded on Laffan's Plain in the Diamond Jubilee Review before the Queen. Also present were the Prince and Princess of Wales, Duke and Duchess of York, Empress Frederick of Prussia, Prince Henry of Battenberg, Indian princes, ministers from the colonies and peers and ambassadors from nearly every state in Europe. Amid all the pomp and circumstance of great military pageants such as this, there was room for other forms of entertainment

offering light relief to the crowds. Redshirt offered the services of his roundabout and sideshows and these soon became regular features at the grand military fêtes.

"There are very few big events that have happened within a radius of four counties that I have not attended," said Redshirt to a local newspaper reporter, "and I think you know of the many big events that I have taken part in at Government House when royalty have 'worked my show'. I mean it, for when the Duke of Connaught was with us the Duchess and the young Princesses relieved me of all responsibility – they bought the whole show, and with the exception of the engine-driver I was quite out of the picture. I've seen princes and princesses, aye, and a king and a queen on my horses. We have been to royal functions at Bagshot Park and in Aldershot. We have fixed up at many a big affair."

Children attending the Camp Coronation fête which took place in the grounds of Government House in 1902 couldn't believe their luck when invited on to Redshirt's roundabouts and swings completely free of charge. They rode on and in them to their hearts' content.[1]

The organisers found Mr Matthews a congenial man to deal with. Used as they were to issuing orders and seeing them carried out, it was good to deal with a showman who had similar command over his troops. They requested him again and again to marshall his amusements at the Grand Military Fêtes held annually to raise money for soldiers' charities.

Government House was a splendid venue. The proceedings were under the immediate patronage of Sir John French who presided in person over the General Committee working diligently for weeks before the actual events. The organisers could call upon hundreds of highly-trained men and the inventive genius of the Royal Engineers to provide novelties of entertainment. From this creative maelstrom emerged cavalry spectaculars involving musical drill or push ball, the torchlight tattoo, and

29

Aldershot Military fête in the grounds of Government House. The Pushball was supplied by A.W.Gamage & Son, of London and Aldershot.

Matthews's Swing boats at the Hampshire & General Friendly Society fête, c1906. The lady in the hat is Mrs Knight, wife of the vice-chairman of the local branch.

balloon ascents. For music they could call upon the bands of a whole Army Corps and Redshirt's fairground organ.

Describing the Fête in July 1904, *Sheldrake's Aldershot Military Gazette* reported:

Many a gap has been filled by Mr Matthews' sideshows, and it was pleasing to find that the steam horses, swings, and all the sideshows were again present at Government House Grounds. To show his appreciation of the object, the proprietor gave £40 of his takings to the cause, and his galloping horses were patronised by quite the élite of the land on both days of the fête.[2]

"Yes," agreed Redshirt later, "I have always tried to do my best for charity, and I suppose I have given hundreds to one cause or another. I've never lost by it, and I know that I have brought credit to my name. I could show you many a letter that you could rightly call an unsolicited testimonial. Lady Audrey Buller was a devoted worker for charity, and she sought my help on many occasions; so did Lord and Lady Pirbright and many more like them who are interested in hospitals, and it's that kind of thing that I like to try and help."[3]

Churches and chapels, too, were included in Redshirt's beneficence. In 1907 he was particularly pleased to be associated with fundraising for the new church being constructed close to his winter-base at North Camp. He took his roundabouts and swings along to a grand fête in the grounds of Government House held on behalf of the endowment fund of St Marks.[4]

Another regular venue was Church Crookham

where Redshirt became a great friend of the vicar, the Reverend Wilfred Wickham, a keen teetotaller who often invited him up to the vicarage for tea. Redshirt annually provided fairground amusements for the Hampshire and General Friendly Society's local Club day in the park of Crookham House (long since demolished), and he also attended the annual Flower Show of Crookham, Crondall and Ewshot Horticultural Society, held in each village by rotation.

For more than thirty years, whenever Redshirt's wagon pulled on to a tober, one of the first things to be produced from its depths was a cage containing a large green and red parrot which, like its owner, was called Polly.

One of the more distant, but nevertheless regular, events attended by the family was Penn Fair in Buckinghamshire on 17 September. Here the lord of the manor, Sir Philip Rose, used to send his gardener to welcome the travellers with gifts of vegetables from his estate and fresh water from the well. There was also the delightful custom of sending down flowers from the garden for the showmen to wear as buttonholes to signal that the fair was open.

Sometimes, choosing a slack moment during the two days' affair, the ladies from the Big House arrived to take tea with Redshirt's family. The parrot on these occasions was not a social asset. Not only was it noisy, it had picked up several inelegant expressions, and so the children got used to rushing with a cloth to cover up its cage.

"Teshilo! Teshilo! Cover up the bird, the ladies is come!" Redshirt would mutter to his grandson.

Tea at Penn Fair. Polly, her daughter, son, and Chap wear flowers sent from the Big House.

"Oh, dordy! Fetch some cups, Amy," her mother would call. She had no need to worry about the state of her china, though. They never bought anything but the very best quality, often Crown Derby, for their own use.

Redshirt's eldest son married Nancy, daughter of Henry Chittock, owner of a travelling Bioscope Show. Both families were present at Penn Fair when it opened on the upper common near Widmer Pond in 1907.[5]

Penn Fair, originally a hiring fair, had by the turn of the century developed into a pleasure fair pure and simple. Showmen usually travelled on from it to Amersham for the nineteenth and thence to High Wycombe. Here took place on 24 September the annual Michaelmas Fair, recognised as one of the oldest and largest hiring fairs still in existence. In 1906 shepherds with tufts of wool in their hair and ploughmen with knots of horsehair and whipcord in their button-holes stood about in groups in the Guildhall hoping to engage themselves to new masters.[6]

Like Chewbacca, the latter-day showmen parked in Fair Meadow viewed these labour transactions with utmost disdain. One man working all his life for other men and selling his birthright – the freedom to come and go as he pleased. No traveller could contemplate that with equanimity. They might consent to hire their services to flatties for a few winter weeks but – once the yellow was on the gorse,

Redshirt with his grandson Coggy at Penn Fair, 1907. Chittock's show in background.

then the road had to open before them, or they might as well be dead.

Huge crowds flocked round the brilliantly lighted booths at Wycombe for two successive evenings in 1907. Confetti battles raged amid scenes of high excitement, but on the third morning the 'Arabs' folded their 'tents' and crept, not quite silently, away.

On 8 February 1908 the Matthews family were clustered in their caravans in Gravel Road, Farnborough. In one wagon lay Redshirt's daughter-in-law, Nancy, having that day given birth to a baby girl. In another lay Redshirt's wife, Polly, fading fast after a lengthy illness. She was seventy-two years old, and in her husband's words:

"One of the best wives God ever gave to man."

They had been together since childhood. When she died four days later, Redshirt was bereft.

"It was a sad day for me when we buried her at Cove cemetery," he recalled, "but though we are only showmen, the sympathy that was shown to me at her death I shall never forget."[7]

It was noticeable that Redshirt's spirits sank in the last months of Polly's illness. The show went on, but clearly his heart was not in it. Organisers of the Richmond Friendly Society fête were not happy about the entertainments he provided in August 1907 and wanted a better array in 1908. Redshirt expressed his regret and vowed he would do his utmost to place new amusements before the public. After some deliberation they decided to accept his tender of £25, secure in the knowledge that at least with him the ground would be left in a proper state after the fête.[8] The ground was left tidy. The fête was a financial success. But people noticed a difference in atmosphere. "There was little life about the thing, and the 'fun of the fair' element seemed very luke warm."[9]

August Bank Holiday Monday, 1909, was cold and grey with intermittent showers. In the Old Deer Park, however, hordes of young people from the suburbs swarmed the roundabouts and filled the swings. In the evening, when naphtha lamps spluttered and electric arc lamps threw their glamour over the crowd, sights and sounds mingled in a rich kaleidoscopic scene. The human spirit is resilient and once more "Here y'ar, al'fun th'fair" rang with conviction.[10] After this there were no more complaints about Redshirt's lack of showmanship.

In July 1910 he supplied a host of sideshows to the Old English Fair held at The Mount, Aldershot, to raise funds for the building of a new hall at St Alban's Church. The following month he provided roundabouts, swings and sideshows for the local Flower Show and Gymkhana.[11]

Chris Odam and his coconut shy.

Gallopers with cockerels taken from Odam's roundabout.

Redshirt's granddaughter at Haslemere Fair, 1911, cooking dinner.

Haslemere Fair, 1911 – watching the shooter.

Business was flourishing and Redshirt had sometimes to make difficult decisions about where best to site his roundabouts.

And then came shocking news. Chris Odam, husband of Polly's sister, had been murdered. Man-Chris, as he was called to distinguish him from Chrissie, his wife, had survived an inauspicious start in life to become a successful showman. His surname was a corruption of Odiham, the village in Hampshire where he had been found abandoned as a child. After his tragic death, his famous steam

roundabout featuring magnificently carved cockerels was brought back to Matthews's yard in Farnborough. It remained for a long while, as if in mourning, under its covers before being sold to Redshirt.

A visitor to the Old Deer Park, Richmond, just before Coronation Day, 1911, was delighted to make the acquaintance of Redshirt's daughter – and the parrot. The bird was in a cage hanging outside her caravan stationed near the steam roundabout. The organ had just struck up an air and the bird was making a curious noise, so the stranger stood staring and listening. The owner of the caravan presently emerged and in response to an enquiry explained that the bird was trying to learn the tune then being played by the organ which was new to it. The tune in question was *Fall in and follow me*. She added that the parrot was over thirty years old, disliked strangers, hated children, and on occasion cried like a baby. There followed a protracted discussion about the merits of caravan-dwelling. And all this time the parrot hung from its ring with its face upraised to the sky as if praying the heavens to fall on this prying stranger. Finally, the gentleman moved away. Whereupon the bird resumed its usual attitude and its study of *Fall in and follow me*.[12]

Coronation Day, 22 June, was celebrated by an Old English fête in the Deer Park.

The things you couldn't do for a penny in that fête weren't worth doing. The modest copper would purchase huge handfuls of confetti, paper mops, cardboard trumpets, sweets, rides on the horses and 'flying cockerels', and scores of similar delights. You could try your skill at hoopla or pose as a temporary

Haslemere Fair, 13 May 1911.

footballer by kicking a ball at long-suffering wooden representations of very 'muddied oafs', you could press the Winchester rifle lovingly against your shoulder and smash a bottle to smithereens ...

The steam organs blared and banged, and to the merry music of such gems as Boiled Beef and Carrots, little groups of men and women tripped it gaily upon the sward, their feet working away so rapidly that they seemed almost to twinkle. Modest-looking young ladies passed you with demure glances, and having proceeded to a safe position behind your back, emptied bagfuls of confetti down your neck, but, bless you, it was no use trying to be cross with them for doing it. The best plan was just to run off and buy some for yourself and take your mirthful revenge.[13]

Suddenly, as if in answer to the parrot's prayer, the heavens opened. By nine o'clock in the evening only a few ardent spirits straggled through the Park in the drenching rain, turning the confetti under foot into a quagmire of red, white and blue. The steam engines still thudded away, the place was ablaze with light, but there were no people. Redshirt still churned out tunes as his riderless horses swung round, more to keep his own spirits up than anything else. His son-in-law, sporadically hitting the wooden pin of the Striker, seemed to have found a harmless way of letting off temper. The only really happy individual was the driver of a large steam engine who unconcernedly climbed onto the top of his machine and spent half-an-hour or more flashing a searchlight over the deserted ground. Whenever he saw a particularly despondent individual he directed the light on to him, just to cheer him up a little.

Despite the weather Redshirt was satisfied. Earlier in the day the Mayor of Richmond had presented him with a silver Coronation Medal and a souvenir tobacco-box in recognition of his services to the borough over the past fifteen years.[14] The parrot was not so happy. On the road back home it became ill and developed a rattle in the throat. "Fetch me some brandy," Redshirt ordered and carefully spooned it into the bird's beak. The parrot shook its feathers appreciatively, but died soon after.

The people of Farnborough, who had delayed their celebrations till the Wednesday following the Coronation, were blessed with glorious summer weather. Hundreds of children from army and civilian families alike marched through the gaily-decorated entrance to Knellwood Park straight to the flagpole where they vigorously voiced three cheers for King and Queen. After that they were free to enjoy all the attractions provided:

And from their point of view the chief of all was Mr W. Matthews's Old English Fair, with its steam galloping horses and wonderful great birds with tail-feathers that must have been the envy of many lady of high and low degree alike. The venerable old showman, a resident of the place, and none more popular than he, had provided the whole fund of his fair, swings, Aunt Sallies, coconuts, and sideshows, so well calculated to please both old and young alike. Mr Matthews was there in person to see that everything was as it should be, and proved a very considerable source of help as a result. [15]

The following week Redshirt attended the Military Coronation fête in Aldershot. Soldiers' children had a high old time of it – with all the rides available to them for the afternoon, free of charge.

Redshirt's roundabout at Cove Green Fair, 1914.

Still in Aldershot, in a meadow in Manor Road 'Ye Olde English Fayre' was held on 18 and 19 July on behalf of St Alban's Church Building Fund. A complete Tudor village had been erected for the occasion – a quadrangle of shops with jettied upper stories, quaint gables and old sloping roofs. Just beyond the 'village gate', somewhat anachronistically, Redshirt had built up his fair. Besides the usual rides and sideshows there was an attraction of a different nature and one that was certainly not Redshirt's idea. The good ladies of Aldershot had constructed a gypsies' encampment, and there they were, all dressed in Zingari costume 'of a most realistic character' living out their fantasies of a free and romantic roaming life. Reluctantly, Redshirt's daughter, Annie, was persuaded to join in the charade; after all, it was all in a good cause. She threw open for inspection (to ladies only) her beautiful wagon, built at a cost of some £500. For one penny, visitors could admire the oil-painted panels, bedroom, sitting-room, and kitchen with bright polished stove adorned with flowers and ornaments. At the same time Redshirt contributed royalties from the steam roundabouts that took on another dimension of charm when filled with smiling ladies in Tudor dress.[16]

During these pre-War years the leisured classes indefatigably organised social events to raise money for 'good causes'. Redshirt proved most amenable when approached by the Aldershot ladies for help in their charitable enterprises.

"Now, if we was to go back afore the Great War," reminisced his daughter Amy, "we used to cater for such grand turn-outs in Government House, yer know. Sometimes only Royalty and suchlike allowed to attend. Like the return of General Buller; well that were celebrated by a great Four Days' Fair. And on the fust day only Royalty and 'ristocrats could come. And our boys, they all wored white trousers. And the money that was collected was all for charity, yer know – boxes and boxes there was of it, carried away at the end of the day by soldiers for the widders and orfens of the campaign. We done the same, too, when the *Titanic* sunk."

In June 1912 Princess Christian opened a bazaar at the Army Service Corps Theatre which raised £426 in two days. Outside the building Redshirt provided over twenty attractions. He, as usual, kept a strict eye on all the proceedings but other members of the family were able to relax and enjoy themselves. For, with the exception of the steam roundabouts, non-commissioned officers had taken over the proprietorship of Redshirt's stalls and for the nonce were vendors of toys, 'Try your luck', 'Have a shot' or 'Roll, Bowl or Pitch' seducers. The incongruity

appealed to 'people of fashion' who, following the lead of Colonel Ford, took the opportunity to ride on the roundabouts with stiff smiles and every suggestion that they were quite used to this sort of thing.[17]

DISTRESSING ACCIDENT AT HIGH WYCOMBE.

TRACTION ENGINE TURNS TURTLE.

GREAT DAMAGE TO SHOWMAN'S STOCK-IN-TRADE.

EMPLOYEE SERIOUSLY HURT.

Upper Hughenden-road, High Wycombe, was the scene of a very distressing accident to Mr. W. Matthews's steam traction engine and roundabout paraphernalia about two o'clock on Sunday afternoon. The vehicles were coming down White Hill, Hughenden

The date was 21 September 1913.

Headlines screamed news of a terrible accident. A traction engine drawing three loads had gone out of control while coming down White Hill, Hughenden, in Buckinghamshire.[18]

Redshirt, after a successful run at Penn and Amersham, was on his way back to High Wycombe for the annual fair and had chosen the Hughenden route to avoid the notoriously dangerous Amersham Hill. It was Sunday afternoon; the time about two o'clock. The procession was headed by a Burrell engine pulling a living wagon, on the front of which sat the showman's eleven year old grand-daughter, Nellie. The little girl heard a pip-pip-pip noise coming from behind them but did not realise anything was wrong until an almighty bang and shrieks tore the air.

What had happened was this. Following them

Accident at High Wycome, 1913.

down the hill was the Savage single-cylinder traction engine *Queen Elizabeth* driven by Redshirt's son. It was pulling three trailers carrying the centre-engine and galloper loads. The driver tried to change to a low gear without first stopping the engine with the result that the locomotive ran out of control and free-wheeled down the hill. Frantic efforts were made to avoid the engine in front by turning towards the side of the road. Running full tilt into the bank the engine turned a complete somersault, pinning driver and mate beneath the wreckage. The centre engine and horse truck were shattered and scattered in all directions.

House-dwellers running to the scene saw scarcely anything for steam and could not get near the wreckage. Thomas Ryan, who had been riding on the centre truck, risked his life to rush forward and pull the driver and steerer from under the traction engine. Then other showmen dived in and out of the steam and clangour, lifting huge weights, to find out whether anyone else was trapped. Fortunately, there was no one else under the huge mass.

The two injured men were carried unconscious and bleeding into a nearby house to await transport to hospital. Meanwhile, news of the fearful accident – the noise had been heard far away – drew great crowds to the scene. A rumbling was heard along the road and this turned out to be Alf Ball's traction engine moving at a furious pace bringing behind it a breakdown gang from the Fair Field. Immediately these workers shot into action. Some went up the hill to clear the way while others tackled the centre piece and its engine which had to be moved before the *Queen Elizabeth* could be lifted. A valuable dynamo was promptly rescued. Then Mayne's traction engine arrived and together the two new engines were able to pull some of the wreckage off the road.

The rear wheels of the centre truck had collapsed, so a fresh carriage was fixed to the back of the vehicle. It was five o'clock before this part of the tackle could be drawn away from the smashed engine. The valves had been broken off when it fell so the steam had soon escaped, but the engine was badly damaged and it was two hours more before it could be dragged away.

Meanwhile the road had been blocked for five hours and thousands of people had come to witness the disaster. Amongst early arrivals were Mr and Mrs Coningsby Disraeli, and in the crowd the whole of the time was poor Redshirt. The public had always been loud in admiration of his equipment, but now their excited attention focussed on the wooden horses and birds strewn with broken legs and broken heads. And his son seriously hurt. It was almost more than he could bear.

High Wycombe Fair went on as scheduled and remained open an extra day to allow showmen to make generous donations to Redshirt as some compensation for his losses. Visitors to Alf Ball's Cinematograph Show were able to see pictures taken by the proprietor at the scene of the crash.

During a lull in the proceedings a reporter for the *South Bucks Standard* interviewed Redshirt and Alf Ball.

'Mr Matthews was profuse in his expressions of thanks to his fellow showmen for their kindness in helping him in his great trouble. Showmen are rivals in business, he said, but they can be, and are, friends, and he could not sufficiently thank those who had helped him.

"Will you tell me," the reporter asked, "whether you are insured or not?"

"You can take it from me that I am insured in no way whatever. Companies are chary of insuring this class of thing."

"What do you estimate the damage at?"

"Well, I should think that to replace it will cost £500 or £600, or perhaps more, for you never can tell. The overturned engine cost me a lot of money to do up only early this year."

"What was the name of the driver of the engine?"

"It was my son and the steerer was a man named Watson."

"If you will not consider it a rude question, Mr Matthews, what is your age?"

"I am 75 [sic] and I am the oldest showman in the Fair. I was the first showman on the ground here in Wycombe. I am a teetotaller, and have been for thirty years. Both the injured men were teetotallers, too. You were there. Did you hear any swear words, or see any man the worse for drink, at all?"'

The reporter confessed that everyone he saw was sober and that he had not heard any language which he did not consider parliamentary. He congratulated Redshirt on looking so tough and well-preserved, and expressed the opinion that he looked like coming to many more Wycombe Fairs yet.

The two injured men recovered after lengthy treatment in the Cottage hospital. Before High Wycombe Fair came round again more momentous events had overtaken the country.

After 1918 Redshirt bought an ex-War Department road locomotive to replace the engine he had lost. He was proud of his Fowler 14113 – naming it *The Lion* – but he ceased travelling so far afield and never resumed his annual visits to Buckinghamshire fairs.

This did not mean, however, that the old man was able to relax his grip on the family business. There was sadly more need than ever for him to shoulder responsibility as a breadwinner. His youngest daughter's husband had died in 1915 as a result of another accident involving one of Redshirt's vehicles. Amy, left to bring up seven chavvies, necessarily relied on her father for support.

Despite such personal tragedies there was a golden sunset glow over Redshirt's last years. In particular he had established a fruitful relationship with the entertainment committees attached to the Royal Military College, Sandhurst. Here, in June 1919 a splendid children's fête was organised.

'Directly the gates opened at 2.45 p.m. an enormous crowd of all ages swept on to the field amid brilliant sunshine and almost oppressive heat. A rush was at once made for the far end, where Mr Matthews of Farnborough, the well-known roundabout proprietor, a lifelong specialist in children's amusements, had gathered a most imposing collection of merry-go-rounds, swing-boats, and sideshows. These were all free to the children until 6pm, and the competition was too keen to allow of much deliberation whether one's mount should be a fiery mustang, a gilded chariot, or a grim but capable-looking ostrich.'[19]

The day was a great success. Redshirt declared that he had carried a greater number of passengers on his roundabouts in a shorter space of time than ever before in all his career as a showman. The reason? The Gentleman Cadets marshalled children on and off the rides with sufficient speed and precision to rejoice the heart of their sergeant-major.

The exercise was repeated to similar acclaim the following year.

In 1921 arrangements were made for a great Gala and fête to raise funds for the College Memorial Chapel. The proceedings on 14 May were opened by an inspection of the Battalion by the Prince of Wales (future King Edward VIII). He went on to the Chapel to examine the work as far as it had proceeded.

After lunch the Prince exchanged his military uniform for a grey lounge suit and visited the 'Village Fair'. His companion, a senior officer of the college, was invited to join the royal guest in a ride on Redshirt's roundabout. In the circumstances he could hardly refuse. The Prince appeared to enjoy himself enormously. The officer, it was rumoured, escaped last stages of *mal-de-mer* by only a matter of seconds.[20] Nearly £6000 was raised by the Gala and fête for the Memorial Chapel. Over £800 of this came from the fair and sideshows. This was one of the many occasions when Redshirt brought credit to his name rather than money into the family purse.

Six months previously Redshirt had been sitting in his wagon in a corner of Aldershot Park when a reporter from the local *Gazette* called to see him.

'The interview took place inside his well-appointed

Redshirt on his wagon steps in Aldershot Park, 1921.

caravan home, a model of comfort and convenience. "A home which," he declared, "I prefer to any built of brick and stone. I first saw the light of day in one, and it is here that I should wish to pass away." A truly wonderful old gentleman is Mr Matthews, and with one exception, the ravages of inexorable time have left no exceptional marks upon him; he suffers in the legs at times, but when these unhappy moments pass you might search the district over and yet fail to find a man so full of life and activity ...

'A simple, unassuming old gentleman, who is nevertheless as remarkably shrewd as any man of business in far more important walks of life ...

"But, don't run away with the idea that it's all honey," insisted Redshirt. "To keep up a show of this kind is a very expensive business. The looker-on may imagine that it's all money coming in, but he would be surprised to see how much has to go out."

Here our friend heaved a sigh that came from his very boots, as he made a casual calculation of the price of petrol, Welsh steam hard, the corn and fodder, labour and wages.

"But," he went on, "what's the use of being worrit. It does no good, but things are now getting a little beyond me and I don't see how one can carry on the way things cost now.'"

The article had concluded:

'It may be, and indeed is, a stern truth that we are living in an age that has multiplied the number of mankind to such an extent that the individual has lost the old characteristics, and old independence, the old morality, and religion if you will, but as I left Mr Matthews I was far from convinced that the old world showman was also quite a thing of the past. He never will be so long as Redshirt Matthews lives, and may his days be even more lengthened.'[21]

It was not to be. Redshirt died in February 1922 in that same caravan, and was buried in the same grave as Polly at Cove.

'Never in the history of Farnborough has there been so remarkable a demonstration at a funeral as that which characterised the burial of the late Mr William Matthews . . .'[22]

The funeral procession, which started away from the fair ground in Peabody Road, was fully a quarter of mile in length, being made up of a dozen carriages and many motor cars. The open hearse seemed a veritable moving bank of magnificent flowers.'

The burial service was conducted at St Mark's church. In his address the vicar remarked:

'Whoever you meet or to whom you may speak, whether he be friend or mere acquaintance, you will realise that there must have been a great feeling of affection and even admiration felt for William Matthews. Our departed friend was noted for his kindliness, his open-handed generosity and for his readiness to assist his fellow men. That is the testimonial you will receive on every hand. He has left us and we will miss his cheery presence ... May each one of us be able to give as good account of our stewardship as we believe William Matthews to have done.'

William and Mary Ann's grave at Cove.

Chapter Six

THESE TURBULENT FAIRS

If you attempt to remonstrate with them woe betide you. You will soon be made to know that this is a chartered fair, that they have erected their stall, caravan or whatnot in the same place for years and years, and that no-one on earth has power to prevent.

(*West Sussex Gazette*, 23 July 1874)

Redshirt and his four brothers lived through a tumultuous chapter in the history of fairfield folk. No more than anyone else could they escape repercussions of the Industrial Revolution. As showmen they exploited the latest inventions to bring new amusements before the public, but at times their profession was hard pressed to survive in a climate conditioned by 'progressive' thinking.

Bognor Fair in 1860 passed with its usual noise, without much display, little quarrelling and no rain. A late harvest gave the field an agreeable smell until the evening shades produced their crop of naphtha flares. The most popular form of rides was provided by donkeys. Apart from these live beasts sinking under their obligation, there were several roundabouts present, pulled round by a pony or pushed into motion by small boys eager to earn free rides for themselves, but these attracted little custom.[1] People wanted something more exciting. One observer concluded that roundabouts had had their day and that the fair itself was doomed. Its decline, he suggested, followed naturally from the advent of cheap railway travel that was bringing more sophisticated attractions such as Crystal Palace within reach.

The public were beginning to find traditional amusements boring. At Portsdown fine weather could still induce many to walk up the hill to see what the annual fair had on offer and then to moan that the booths afforded but inferior accommodation and only rubbish was being vended. One gentleman lamented the absence of Wombwell and said that the shows looked worn out, as if going with the fair which was undoubtedly declining.[2] He reckoned without the resilience and innovative genius of travelling showmen.

Chichester's annual Sloe, oft-times dubbed 'Slough', Fair was notorious for its wet weather. In October 1863 there was a larger than usual turn out of roundabouts, including one ambitiously fitted with

canvas for shelter – one of the first 'tilts' recorded on such a ride.[3] Nevertheless, the roundabouts still depended on muscle power – human or equine – to propel them. Such limitations were about to be surmounted.

At Brighton's Holy Thursday Fair in 1865 there were shooting galleries and oyster barrows, ten toy stands, six drinking booths, four gingerbread stalls, three swings and two roundabouts, one of which was provided with … 'a perfect Pegasus which snorted steam'! Even a peepshow illustrating the examination of Miss Constance Kent and the assassination of President Lincoln could not compete with the marvel of a roundabout driven by steam![4]

The following year at Brighton's August Races crowds gazed awestruck at 'run rounds' turned by steam and barrelled organs set in action by steam.[5] Visitors to Hambledon Hunt Steeple Chases in 1868 were similarly astounded by the new contraptions:

'The horses were very smartly painted; and the entire decoration of the concern was very showy in its way, with looking glasses and other ornamentation. A ride on these gay steeds only costs one penny. Instead of the 'run round' being turned by men as in olden times, a small steam engine does the work. The boiler of the engine is fed by buckets of water standing by; it costs but little for fire; and the tiny engine works about with a vigour and smartness quite amusing to witness. Not only does it drive the 'turn round' but it sets an organ in motion, and also by a touch gives forth the shrillest of whistles, just to keep the game going. The whole affair is very complete, and the toy engine is called *The Little Wonder*.'[6]

Showmen had harnessed steam for the delight of their public. At the same time development of steam-driven traction engines was giving promise of greater mobility for heavy loads, although their use on the roads was hampered by prohibitive tolls. Then, just at the moment when travelling showmen were poised on the threshold of their own technological revolution, their profession came under bitter attack. Fairs were increasingly regarded as uncomfortable anachronisms in the new urbanised society. In 1871 the Fairs Act gave the Secretary of State powers of abolition on the grounds that fairs were unnecessary, encouraged grievous immorality and were injurious to the inhabitants of the towns where they were held. The Act expressed a real sense of grievance felt in the country at large. Redshirt and his brothers played unwitting parts in the sort of events that fuelled criticism of fairs and were involved in clashes between local authorities and showmen which inevitably followed.

The first charge made against fairs in the 1871 Act was that they were 'unnecessary'. Many of the annual fairs frequented by the Matthews family had been in existence since the Middle Ages, so what had happened to make their existence questionable in the mid-nineteenth century? A trip to Rogate Fair held annually on 27 September provides part of the answer.

Rogate Fair reputedly originated in a grant by Ralph de Camvis in 1290. Until the beginning of the nineteenth century it was a cattle fair, but then periodical markets in neighbouring towns took over this role and it lived on as a lively pleasure fair. Old customs attached to the event were cherished. Rogate people felt it essential to have a pork joint on fair day so, days before, pigs ran squealing from the knife. Then, at an early hour on the twenty-seventh the air was redolent with appetising cooking smells, two spits being kept turning throughout the day at the White Horse Inn. Meanwhile, an anxious eye was kept on the weather which, melancholy fact, was traditionally wet. In 1862 one cheerful soul sang:

> *Twas wet in the morning*
> *Just to keep up the Charter;*
> *But the clouds cleared away,*
> *And 'twas much finer arter.*[7]

Besides the usual stalls, there was dancing at the public houses till nearly midnight. One band in 1859 comprised two cornets and one sax tuba and their softest music was supposedly marked '*fff*', but the festivities passed off peacefully with not the slightest robbery or the sound of a rams-horn word.[8]

Rogate people seemed particularly fond of their fair and held a warm place in their hearts for the showmen who provided the annual amusements. In 1877, it was quoted:

As usual a good number of the gipsy [sic] tribe were present with their various inducements to extract the coppers from the juvenile population of the district, a roaring trade being done by the proprietor of a horse-roundabout ... A word for the gipsies – we hear all left the place in quite as respectable a manner as this class of people generally do, and on the next morning by ten a.m. they had all vanished.[9]

If, at Rogate, the original purpose of the fair, that of a cattle market, had been eroded, it lived on vigorously as a pleasure fair, valued as a social occasion. Nevertheless, even at Rogate people were delighted when the occasion passed without incidents involving robbery or 'rams-horn' words. It was sadly true that fairs were associated with drunkenness, brawling, gambling, cheating and robbery, as will be seen if we follow the travellers on to other annual fairs on their circuit in the decades before and after the Fairs Act.

At the time when stock fairs were being eclipsed by competition from regular country markets they were dramatically weakened by the effects of cattle plague in 1867. At Crawley May Fair prohibition of neat stock was reflected in the thin attendance.[10] On the other hand at St George's Fair held in East Street, Chichester, a year later there was a larger than usual gathering. The additional novelty of a roundabout proved attractive especially with the young people and the Militia.[11] The October Sloe Fair held in Freeland's Field, Northgate, was also larger than normal, with a good supply of horses but scarcely any hops; hops being nearly a thing of the past at this fair now.[12]

Opposition to fairs moved easily from a charge that they were no longer necessary to criticism of their attendant vices. About twenty-eight thousand sheep and lambs were still being penned at Lindfield Fair in 1862. There was little business done in the horse fair. What did attract attention was the number of Cockney sellers of rings and brooches gulling the yokels of their shillings.[13] At Horsham's Winter Colt Fair held in the Bishoprick in 1869 the unsuspecting were liable to be taken in by two notorious forms of swindling. Who could resist the purchase of a brand new purse complete with its contents of three half crowns, all for the price of one shilling? It sounded too good to be true, and of course it was.

It is laughable as it is surprising to see with what eagerness and curiosity these poor dupes open their purse after having parted with their shilling – perhaps the last – to see what it contains; and when they discover that there are only two or three half-pence for them, and are told by the gabbler on his perch that they were a set of silly yokels for not purchasing at the right time – the moment the half crowns are put into the purse – they actually seem to enjoy the bait, and if another shilling can be found, they are uneasy until they have parted with it.[14]

While this business was going on, in a different part of the fair another very old trick was being practised. A respectably dressed 'gentleman' selected a victim and pointed out to him a fine, showy horse that he was anxious to purchase. Unfortunately, being known to the dealer as a gentleman, he was afraid of being made to pay over the odds if he attempted to make the deal himself. He offered his new friend a generous two sovereigns to buy the animal on his behalf for anything up to £35. The commissioned man quickly managed the transaction, proffered a cheque in payment, but the dealer who had been induced to part with such a fine horse for £32.10s. would take nothing but gold. A visit to the bank procured the necessary and the deal was completed. Nothing remained but to find the 'gentleman' for whom the horse was purchased. How strange when he was nowhere to be found; but then, not so strange when closer inspection revealed the horse to be a broken-winded nag scarcely worth buying at any price! A woman who ventured into a beershop had her pocket cut clean off and a gentleman sauntering on the railway station platform was eased of his gold watch and chain. All these and more were incidents unconnected with showmen, but they happened on fair day and therefore brought the fair into disrepute.

Crawley May Fair in 1865 provides a vision of what it was like for people living in the town suddenly to have a fair in their midst.

'Our May Fair took place amid beautiful sunshine on Monday last, and judging by the crowded state of our little town, it was evidently a successful one, at any rate in a commercial point of view. The early train brought all who were interested in the fair who had not come by road, who, after a glass of ale and a clean shave launched into the market to pinch bullocks and converse on the several merits or faults of the assembled stock – some buying and others selling.

'The pleasure fair was well patronised by old and young, and the proprietors of the *Rouge et Noir* tables, roulette and racing boards, must have reaped a rich harvest from the smock frock gentry – and the spirited manager of the royal wax work seemed to be making a *petite* fortune by exhibiting the effigies of his prince and princess, moulded in delicate, though rather bilious-looking wax; a professor of natural history by inviting the world to view his six-legged lamb, four-legged duck and several other curiosities of nature, together with an enormous rat, which, judging

from the painting outside, must have shrunk considerably since he sat for his portrait, evidently went away with much heavier pockets.

'A peepshow located in the middle of the fair ought to have been crushed by the arm of the law, the dirty dressed and dirtier minded owner exhibiting in broad daylight to the youths of Crawley the most indecent photographs that Holywell Street could produce, and there is no doubt but that many respectable persons paid their humble fee (1d) little suspecting by the outside – a gold and vermilion saloon – that such a sight awaited them, causing them to exclaim with Avon's Swan: "O, that deceit should dwell in such a gorgeous palace."

'Knock-'em-downs were doing a brisk trade, and nuts were offered as prizes to the lovers of the gun, and everyone seemed to be going in for thorough enjoyment. Dancing commenced with the dusk and was continued till a late hour, Hebe being in constant attendance upon Terpsichore.'

Hebe had a lot to answer for when it came to the immorality and excesses associated with fairs. Cat-on-Hill fair was notorious for its preceding 'Tap-up-Sunday', when the road from Guildford to St Catherine's Hill swarmed with itinerant vendors of beer, and drunkenness was the rule rather than the exception. In October 1863 the customary chestnut fight developed into full-scale riotous melée that left thirty people injured.[15] In 1874 the New Licensing Act prohibiting sale of intoxicants after ten o'clock curbed the old habits and the midnight orgies of past years were averted.

Fairs were a platform for so many vices in Victorian society and denounced accordingly. At the same time active measures were being taken to reinforce law and order. In Petworth the exertions of the admirable Superintendent Kemmish usually kept the excitement within acceptable bounds at fair time, but the bill incurred by extra policing was left to be picked up by local residents and tradesmen.

The Fairs Act of 1871 specified that fairs were injurious to the inhabitants of the towns where they were held. Chichester's May Fair was a great nuisance to tradesmen because the stalls in East Street were pitched close to the pavements and impeded the traffic. At Littlehampton, Surrey Street traffic was always obstructed when the annual fair was in progress.

At Bognor in 1874 the town fair was castigated as:

Men with hoarse voices and sunburnt females encouraging their fellow creatures to throw away strength and money at the knock-'em-downs, dust, glare, noise, discord, gingercake and gingerbeer, all that has been and will be at such a time a source of profit to vendors and a cause of regret to small shopkeepers, a pleasure to many and a nuisance to some. Still the stalls of 'limited liability' where a penny invested will secure a 'fairing' must be a step in the direction of economy; and these are and were much patronised. The fair tells you that the longest day of the year is past and that Goodwood Races is nigh at hand. [16]

Besides traffic disruption, unwelcome competition with local traders, noisy disturbance, there was the prospect of messy streets to be cleared up afterwards and possible health hazards. Accidents arising from knock-'em-downs and shooting galleries were rife, and the greater velocity of steam-driven roundabouts produced new dangers. Naphtha flares were obvious fire risks, as seen at Sloe Fair in 1865 when a shooting gallery went up in flames and was destroyed within minutes.[17]

All these problems vexed municipal authorities enthusiastically launched on paths of reforming, reorganising and regulating their boroughs. Fairs were an infernal nuisance, yet with what incredible obstinacy the public clung to their so-called pleasures. On the other hand no one could ignore proven threats to environmental health. One of the most perilous charges made against travellers was that they were disease-carriers; nothing was so guaranteed to turn the settled population against them.

5 July 1871 dawned wet and blustery, but this did not prevent people thronging to the first day of Bognor Fair. Then rumour whispered that the fair-keepers had brought smallpox with them into town. In a moment the crowds vanished, leaving the streets deserted. The showmen hastily consulted together and sent round the Town Crier to offer a reward of £5 for information leading to those who had perpetrated the hoax, but nothing could remedy the situation. The fair was ruined.[18]

Horsham was the venue for four great annual fairs in the nineteenth century: Teg Fair fixed to date 5 April, Lamb Fair 18 July, St Leonard's Fair 17 November and Winter Colt Fair 27 November. The fairs brought a lot of trade into the town, but much upheaval too. In 1872 the July Lamb and Pleasure Fair attracted a string of complaints from residents:

The continual thumping into an old broken drum and clamour of a couple of cracked trumpets, plus the odour tends to drive a man out of his mind. There is no way of getting rid of these noisy and filthy people till after midnight. [19]

The trouble was that sometimes Horsham's Pleasure Fair enjoyed an extended run. It was scheduled to take place on the Saturday following the Lamb Fair but when, as in 1874, the business fair occurred on a Saturday, the town was treated to what was called a nine days' fair:

i.e. those who live around Gaol Green have the annoyance, or privilege, of seeing, hearing, or smelling a lot of carts, tents, or fever dens pitched about in this open space for those blessed nine days (the two Saturdays more particularly) the owners or occupiers of the tents think nothing of pitching one of their machines close up to the pavement directly in front of one's office or place of business, shutting you out entirely from the view of casual customers, and if you attempt to remonstrate with them woe betide you. You will soon be made to know that this is a chartered fair, that they have erected their stall, caravan, or whatnot in the same place for years and years, and that no-one on earth has power to prevent . . . It is impossible to avoid feeling sore when we reflect on our littleness and incapacity to remove what must be considered by everyone who has any respect for morality, decency and comfort, as an intolerable nuisance. [20]

Chorley Matthews, Redshirt's younger brother.

A tilt-cart belonging to Chorley.

There was more than irritation at being inconvenienced behind this angry tirade. There was fear of contagion. Chorley Matthews, Redshirt's younger brother, had arrived at the fair with his wife, Phoebe, about to give birth to their fourth child. Under a mound of blankets in their covered cart two of their other children, both little girls, lay huddled together sweating with fever. On the Monday three-year old Carrie died. The authorities were outraged. As the little corpse was hurried off to the grave, the other child was despatched to the Union Hospital. Chorley's tilt-cart was seized, fumigated and sent away out of the town.[21] Within a month a petition from the residents of Gaol Green was presented to the Magistrates asking them to limit the July Pleasure Fair to one day. The Duke of Norfolk, as owner of the fair, was approached and offered no objection. The Magistrates made formal application to the Secretary of State and the desired changes were made.[22]

Another of Redshirt's brothers, Harelip Matthews, was involved in something like a riot at Horsham's Teg Fair in 1883. The Local Board decided that the time had come to take a stand and instructed the police to prevent showmen building up on Gaol Green in the Carfax. Half an hour after midnight on 4/5 April Harelip, his father-in-law Jack Harris, Henry Carter, and John Smith came down North Street, each leading a horse and wagon. The officers watched them come. Opposite the *Hurst Arms* PC Robinson intercepted Jack Harris.

"You will not be allowed to take your carts on to the Green," he announced.

"I shall go and you may do what the ... you like," Jack said. The constable seized the horse's bridle. Jack struck out right and left. One hand caught Robinson's mouth, the other knocked off PC Firman's helmet. The constables gave way muttering that summonses would follow.

And so, later that morning:

The customary following of house-cart wanderers, who travel from fair to fair with roundabouts, swings, rifle-shooting galleries etc. assembled on the Green with their carts and apparatus, taking preliminary steps for putting their places in order, but were warned at the same time by an officer of the Local Board that if they attempted to occupy the Green in the way they proposed they would be summoned.

Nevertheless, after a consultation had been held on the Green with the several proprietors of these intolerable nuisances, the rougher following in connection with them were set to work building up their places, and in a very short time everything was put in motion, wooden balls and coconuts were flying about in all directions, and with the assistance of a barrel organ and a bell, which constituted a band of music for the lot of them, there was a regular hurly-burly from one end of the Green to the other and discordant and unearthly noises enough to drive any total abstainer to break his pledge.[23]

Of course the matter did not end there. The travellers were riled. Several times during the day Harelip's brother-in-law had to be cautioned by the police for threatening behaviour. Eventually they decided to arrest him.

"Will you go to the station quietly?" they asked.

"Yes," he said, and immediately bolted into the Carfax and hid himself in one of the wagons. A violent struggle ensued. For a brief moment Harris was rescued by fellow travellers, but with the arrival of reinforcements the police apprehended their man again and dragged him off to the lock-up.

The following week Jack Harris, Harelip Matthews, Henry Carter and John Smith were charged with offences under the Towns Police Clauses Act – to wit, having erected various exhibitions on the Gaol Green, contrary to notice given them. Mr Cotching for the Local Board said they had no desire to inflict penalties on any of the defendants; what they really wanted was a decision from the Bench as to whether these people had any legal right to erect their machinery where they did. As the cases were all similar he suggested they select one only as a test case, and Jack Harris was selected for this privilege. The court was then adjourned for a week.

In the interval the Local Board made frantic research into possible precedents, with the following result:

Mr Cotching asked leave of the Bench to withdraw any summons against Jack Harris, as the Board had decided not to pursue the matter any further for the moment.

"That's all very well," grumbled the police superintendent, "but what about the assault carried out on my men?"

Well, as at the time the alleged assaults happened the constables were acting under the orders of the Local Board, and as that Local Board had no power to interfere with the showmen, the officers could not have been injured 'whilst in the execution of their duty.' Jack Harris was found guilty of the less serious crime of common assault and was fined five shillings.[24] It was a lesson to the Local Board who resorted to more diplomatic means of solving their problems. In 1885 the fair was moved with the showmen's consent to the Cattle Market in the Bishoprick, much to the delight of the inhabitants of the Carfax and Gaol Green.[25]

The Fairs Act so far as showmen were concerned represented the cloudy side of a picture, on the other side of which the sun still shone. Contemporary nostalgia for Ye Olde England led to efforts to restore ancient customs of the countryside. In 1864 Ebernoe Horn Fair in Sussex was revived after many years neglect.

The day was ushered in by rather heavy showers of rain; however, as the morning wore on, the rain ceased, the clouds dispersed, and the misty vapour that enveloped the fair face of nature gradually rolled away towards the distant downs.

This auspicious change in the weather soon brought together a large number of spectators; tents, booths, and stalls rose as if by magic.

There was also an elegant little marquee erected for the use of W. Peachey Esq. (the Lord of the Manor) and guests, which was filled at different times of the day by an elegant assemblage of ladies and gentlemen, who appeared to take the liveliest interest in all that was going on. One of the most conspicuous objects of interest was the roasting of the horned sheep in the open air. A large group was gathered round this particular spot, and notwithstanding the intense heat of the fire could not tear themselves away from the seething and sputtering object of their admiration.[26]

Soon, every year to Ebernoe Horn Fair came a burly figure walking alongside his loaded pony. He unpacked poles and wooden stands, unhitched two coarse sacking bags from either side, then he lifted off the bulky grey canvas that protected the pony's back from rubbing. After hammering in the poles, he strung the canvas between them to form a backcloth. From one of the bags he picked out coconuts and carefully balanced them on stands. From the other bag he tipped a pile of short wooden sticks to be used as missiles.

As the fair opened, the voice of Andrew Smith at his coconut sheet could be heard to holla:

"Step up! Step up! Every one a good 'un!"

And his voice continued to holla that refrain at Ebernoe Horn Fair for over seventy years.

Chapter Seven
ANDREW WITH HIS COCONUT SHIES

He was patronised by Queen Victoria at Windsor Fair when it was held in the Windsor High Street, and on more than one occasion by members of Foreign Royalty and by noble families. To rich and poor alike he was 'just Andrew with his coconut shies'.
(*West Sussex Gazette*,18 March 1937)

Andrew Smith had been born in a tent at Ore, near Hastings, in Sussex, on 30 December 1851, and he spent the rest of the century travelling the roads of southern England in a pattern trodden by generations of his ancestors. His father, John Smith, was an itinerant basket-maker whose family claimed to have figured on fairgrounds for more than three hundred years, and his mother, Prissy, née Dean, became the redoubtable fizzer-seller at Aldershot Camp after marrying William Bowers as her second husband. Before his death in 1937 Andrew had carved out a place for himself in Sussex folklore.

Stout, but sturdy, with short arms, clenched fists – Andrew always looked the same, always was the same, a law unto himself. "Every one a good 'un!" he would roar from his perch on a backless wooden chair. He had his customary pitch at every annual fair he visited, and on no account would he allow himself to be moved from that position.

Andrew had a very distinctive way of speaking – especially when roused. Innocent-seeming, quiet words slipped tonelessly through lips that he had clamped together in a thin straight line. "So, you've got 'ere first, mush – have yer?" he would whisper to a rival showman. "And now you've built up yer stuff on Andrew's pitch. Hmm, I see." Normally he straightway threw down his hat and started stripping off jacket and wesket. If he didn't, this was no cause for complacency. On one occasion Andrew pulled into a field to find a rival had erected a sideshow on his own customary pitch. After a quiet exchange of words, the fellow still refused to budge. Andrew turned away in disgust and fell to building up his coconut shy on another site – right across the only gate into the fairground. Of course, the other travellers loved it, "laughed, some of 'em, till they was bustin." But Andrew was not smiling so, if anyone was to take money that day, the menfolk had to sort

Andrew Smith.

out the offender, who was soon dismantling his sideshow and sheepishly building up elsewhere.

Because he opened many of the old Charter Fairs and fought for their prerogatives, Andrew Smith was known as 'Charter Showman of the South of England'. He was particularly associated with Petworth's Winter Fair, attending it regularly for more than eighty years.

This fair originally took place on Egdean Common but, despite opposition, moved to Petworth in 1839. Thereafter, the stock fair was held on Hamper's Common, while the pleasure fair took over the principal streets of the town. Year after year the local newspaper, after reporting on the fluctuating fortunes of the stock trade, inveighed against the turmoil caused by the 'roughs' who swarmed into town for the pleasure fair. In 1856 police were kept on the alert till one o'clock in the morning, at which hour there was a general mêlée ending only when two lively gentlemen were 'shopped up'.[1]

Ten years later cattle plague almost put paid to the stock fair but the pleasure fair was thriving. Mr Superintendent Kemmish was on the alert, ready to reap his rich annual yield of drunks, thieves and rowdies. In 1868 he brought to book a vendor of nuts at the fair, for 'ringing the changes'; that is, swindling people by giving and retracting a succession of coins in their change.[2]

Andrew was a horse-dealer as well as showman, and he sold several fine beasts on Hamper's Common in 1894 at one of the last fairs to be held on that site. He also sold horses at the last fair to be held in Midhurst. Held annually on 29 October, as a stock fair it declined from the 1860s onwards. However, it remained a popular engagement for travellers, not least for the chance it gave their families to gather up chestnuts in Cowdray Park; they brought back sacksful ready for roasting or boiling in salt water for a meal. Midhurst Fair went into sharp decline in the early years of the twentieth century, and it was remarked in 1908 that 'to the annoyance of the residents a very queer assortment of van-dwellers took possession of the Square about mid-day, but they did very little business.'[3] In the eighteenth century one of the largest cattle fairs in Sussex took place annually on 11 December in the village of Bolney. Bough houses for the temporary sale of beer were erected on the common and drovers arrived from as far afield as Wales and Ireland with their beasts. After Bolney Common was enclosed, the fair was transferred to East Grinstead. Andrew regularly visited this fair to trade horses, running them through the crowds to show their paces until the police suppressed the dangerous practice in 1881.

Andrew was present at the last charter fairs to be held in the towns of Haslemere, Crawley and Guildford, and fought any changes made in showmen's customary rights to the bitter end. On the other hand there were changes in the countryside which he welcomed. No one knew better all the pay-gates and toll-bars in Sussex, and Andrew celebrated when in 1866 so many of them, including those at Cuckfield, Scaynes Hill, Newick, Piltdown and Buxted were abolished. So far as he was concerned the sooner the whole lot were done away with the better, maintaining that he had in the course of one day's travelling with his fair occasionally paid as much as ten pounds in tolls.

When Charley Lee turned up at Petworth in

February 1876 to answer a charge of assault brought by Andrew Smith, he was left waiting at the court until it was obvious that the plaintiff was not going to appear. The case was dismissed.[4] But Andrew did not get off so lightly in June the following year when charged in the same court with committing an assault at Kirdford Club Festivities.

Andrew's wife, Amy, four months gone with child, had been looking after the coconut-shy when insulted by another woman traveller. Soon they were rolling together, kicking and scratching on the ground. Amy caught hold of the other woman's hair while Andrew kicked her in the side; 'though without doing her much hurt', it was stated in court. Andrew was fined ten shillings.[5]

The following month he had to hand over half a sovereign at Midhurst Petty Sessions for allowing his travelling cart to obstruct the highway at Lodsworth.[6] Andrew's winter-quarters were at Godalming at this time and it was there that his son, Tom, was born in November. The baby was christened in the local church, with his father's occupation being recorded as 'hawker'. Ten years later Andrew was described as a 'traveller' living at Godalming, when he appeared in Lewes Court to press charges of assault against Fred Harris.[7]

Fred, son of Jack Harris, had his headquarters at Chailey. Andrew and Amy stopped there on their way from Ebernoe to Uckfield in July 1887. Before setting out from Chailey, according to Andrew's evidence, he met Harris who, without any provocation, beat him with a stick and kicked him. Amy Smith corroborated her husband's story. Two witnesses called by the defendant presented a different picture. Andrew Smith began the row, they said, by shouting and cussing at Harris and both Smiths appeared to be very drunk. The magistrates dismissed the case with the weary remark that complainant and defendant seemed as bad as each other.

In September 1899 Andrew and Amy, on their way to Midhurst with their son Thomas, camped on Henley common for a couple of nights with three vans plus swings, roundabout, shooting gallery and a total of eight horses. They were described as van-dwellers who attended fêtes and galas. A year later found Andrew back on Henley common, this time with his eight children and travelling with five vans drawn by seven horses. Having come from Midhurst, they were on their way to High Buildings, Fernhurst. Henley was clearly a good stop-over place, because in July 1901 Andrew, Amy and their children spent another couple of nights there on their way from Sidlesham to Ebernoe fair.

A minor brush with the law in June 1902 saw

Andrew brought before the Petworth Petty Sessions charged with trespass in search of conies.[8] A week later he was plaintiff at Chichester, having summoned Redshirt's brother, Harelip, before the County Bench to show cause why he should not provide sureties to keep the peace. The case arose over disputed pitches at Selsey Club and Andrew's solicitor introduced his client as 'a travelling showman attending fairs, clubs, etc. with swings' and as 'a man well-known in the district who bore an excellent character; which could, if necessary, be spoken to by the police.' After Andrew, Amy and their daughter had all testified to the threats and shocking bad language used by Harelip, Constable Avis also spoke to the annoyance caused to Smith by Matthews, who pitched his show on Smith's ground. The policeman went on to describe Andrew as a 'peaceable' man. Harelip was bound over and had to pay costs.[9] Andrew must have left court that day with a rare smile on his face.

The Matthews family were seething; just biding their chance for revenge. It came a few weeks later at Lodsworth Club where a pitched battle took place between the rival clans that brought members of both families into court. All the trouble-makers were bound over in the sum of a hundred pounds each to keep the peace.[10] Although by 1903 Andrew had set up new headquarters in Nutbourne, near Emsworth, he still spent most of his time on the road. On 15 May he stopped for four nights with his wife, eight children, six vans and seven horses on private ground in Chapel Street, Fernhurst, on their way from Haslemere to Bosham, but when, ten days later, he and Amy built up their roundabout at Littlehampton Fair they unwisely pitched on a site usually taken by Kate Lee. Result? While Amy was handing a pole up to Andrew, Kate ran upon her with an iron stake threatening to beat her brains out.

"Send yer daughters out an' I'll do the same for them," she screeched.

At this juncture sweeter reason prevailed. Another traveller wrenched the stake from Kate's hand, allowing her pause to pull herself together before squaring her fists and coming in to fight in more civilised fashion. Amy discreetly disappeared into her wagon. Whereupon Kate, all the while muttering dire threats, hitched up her van and lodged it underneath Andrew's roundabout, preventing it from being turned.[11] Harting Fair, November 1904, was scene of a similar fracas. This time Andrew had built up his roundabout on a pitch occupied the year before by Dicky Wall. Predictably Wall responded by getting his men to back carts into Andrew's show. Andrew took off his jacket and wesket and would have weighed in had not PC Hills intervened.[12]

Interestingly, what brought the matter into court were the epithets applied by Job Matthews, swing attendant, to Andrew and his daughter. Andrew never could abide bad language and to hear his good self and his daughter so described in a public place was more than he would tolerate. The Bench was some time in consultation before deciding to dismiss the case against Job – but then the latter possessed a certain charm when it came to dealing with the law, as the following two incidents will show.

When brought before the Chichester County Bench charged with letting his van obstruct the highway and two horses stray thereon, Job, clearly puzzled, turned the questioning so that he could interrogate the constable.

"Was I in the wagon when you came to me?"

"Yes."

"Didn't I ask you to have a cup of tea?"

"Yes."

Job had established the fact that he and the constable were on equal, nay friendly, terms. The case proceeded with Job and his wife bowing and curtseying to the Bench, volubly interrupting the evidence throughout. Eventually came a clear question:

"How do you plead?"

"Oh, quite guilty," Job replied.

The fine and costs amounted to £1.4s.6d.

"'eart-achin'," his wife called it, and was all for going to prison instead, but Job, with a smile, paid up and scarpered.[13]

Then, in 1905 at Littlehampton, a constable approached Job's wagon only to draw back when the black lurcher underneath the steps growled menacingly.[14]

"Don't be afeared, the dog won't hurt yer," said Job.

"Well, I've had complaints and I've come to see your licence for him," said the constable.

"Dordy," says Job, "but that dog don't belong ter me. I've never seen it afore in me life, s'truth."

At Sloe Fair that autumn Job was present with his swings and Andrew with his coconut shy, their old sores healed over. The event attracted bigger crowds than for many years past.

Everybody, high and low, seemed to be gone to swell the crowd on those noisy acres, where the whirligigs whirled, and the steam sideshows hooted their raucous invitations, and 'all the fun of the fair' was forced upon one at every turn by insistent hawkers of little tubes of water, which it was the correct thing to squirt down your neighbour's neck, or into her eye ... One of the best known frequenters of the fair, Andrew

Smith, met with a nasty accident as he was leaving the city with one of his caravans on Saturday morning. He had a collision in Orchard Terrace with another vehicle, and was thrown off under the wheels of his caravan, which passed over his chest, breaking his collarbone, and severely crushing him. He was driven to the Infirmary where he remains, but his condition is not regarded as serious.[15]

Clearly not. Severely crushed he may have been, but he had sufficiently recovered to be driving a horse and cart while under the influence of drink at Petworth a fortnight later.[16]

In 1907 a case was brought against him, not by one of his rival showmen, but by his wife. In the course of her evidence Amy accused Andrew of pulling her out of bed in her wagon when she was far from well, hitting and jumping on her, and threatening her with a loaded gun. What was more, she said, she had had cause to summon him at Staines, Guildford, Petworth and Chichester and on all these occasions he had been bound over and fined for knocking her about. Andrew's contention that it was her own persistent drunkenness which caused the quarrels Amy vigorously denied.

This sorry record of the couple's matrimonial difficulties occupied the Magistrates for a long time, and it was fortunate for Andrew that he was able to find another friendly policeman to testify to his good character – well, Superintendent Ellis of Chichester gave him a good character 'barring his family affairs.' (After all, it wasn't Andrew's fault if his extended family included nearly every fairground traveller in the south of England.)

When Amy went on to seek a separation order, she was asked what her husband's profits would amount to on average throughout the year. "Nine or ten pounds a week," she replied. The Bench, after a private consultation, imposed a fine of ten shillings and costs for the assault, and granted a separation order with maintenance at twelve shillings a week.[17] Whatever the magistrates' concern, their solution for the problem was short-lived. Andrew and Amy were soon back together again, loving and abusing, abusing and loving each other as before.

In June 1908 Andrew was summoned by the police for causing an obstruction with seven wagons in the streets at Bosham. Andrew stood in court and roundly declared that the occasion was Bosham Fair and that he had put his wagons on the spot complained of for forty years, as had his father and mother before him. His solicitor suggested that a prosecution could not be sustained for obstructing a highway by holding a fair that had existed

immemorially.

"But," queried the Bench, "can one man hold a fair?"

When that man was Andrew Smith, it appeared he could.[18]

Superintendent Ellis decided not to press the case. Instead, he took Andrew aside for a little chat. Agreement was reached. In future Andrew would draw his wagons into a field for 'Bosham Fair'. The matter ended peacefully; it was so much better to work with Andrew Smith, than against him. However, like the prophet, least honoured in his own land, as paterfamilias Andrew commanded less than complete respect.

There was a family disagreement at Lodsworth Club Day in 1909. Tongues, hands and feet being found insufficient to express differences, poles and hammers were requisitioned and a free-for-all commenced.[19]

Tom Smith.

The trouble started at about eleven o'clock at night when the fair was over and Andrew asked Edward Carter, a fellow traveller, for seven shillings and sixpence owing to him. Carter replied by knocking the old man down. Up rushed Andrew's son, Tom, arms flailing, not to hit Carter, but to take the opportunity to kick his father as he lay on the ground.

Estate Office.
Petworth.   29ᵗʰ May
                                    1911

M⸴ Andrew Smith agrees to
bring his Swing Boats Hoop la
Cocoa Nut Shies, shooting Gallery, Aunt Sally &c.
to Petworth Park on Coronation
day June 22ᵈ 1911 – He is
to be paid the sum of Seven
pounds and to let the Children
have free swings from the morning
until three o'clock in the
afternoon, after that time he
is to charge for rides in the
usual way –

His
                    Andrew + Smith
Witness Geo⸴ Wilson   Mark

Andrew's contract with the Leconfield Estate Office.
Below: 1.Andrew Smith 2.Henry Cogger 3.Jim Smith
(lad) 4.Chorley Matthews 5.Tom Smith.

Meanwhile, Carter was punching Andrew's other son, Joe, and it was to protect her husband that Esther Smith joined in the fray. She was immediately knocked down with a hammer by Mary Ann Smith, who was the wife of Tom. And then Rosa, Andrew's daughter, was hit by Tom, to teach her for interfering.

The sequel was the appearance of practically all the party, with the addition of Amy to give evidence on her husband's behalf, at Midhurst Petty Sessions. All the defendants were fined one pound each plus costs. Tom Smith and Edward Carter – much to Andrew's satisfaction – were also fined for using bad language.

Andrew had now established his winter-quarters at Strood Green, near Petworth. He was eager to exploit special opportunities for providing amusements at public celebrations of the coronation of King George V in 1911, and agreed to open his stuff in Petworth Park on 22 June after arranging with the Leconfield Estate Office that he would, in return for a lump sum, give free rides for children until three o'clock in the afternoon.

"Every one a good 'un!" rang out from his coconut shy and people flocked to try their luck, not drawn by the prizes so much as the magnetism of Andrew. Unchanging, uncompromising, inimitable Andrew had become a human landmark at local events. His suits he commissioned from Mrs Thompson, wife of the storekeeper in Kirdford, and they had to be cut from special heavy-duty cloth to a pattern already archaic, and he was never seen, summer or winter, without his black bowler hat.

Like all travellers, he had a soft spot for chavvies, beckoning them closer and closer to the coconuts if they couldn't hit one from the statutory distance. It often rained during Petworth's November Fair. One year a tiny girl was having no success at all at Andrew's stall. He made her stand almost close enough to touch the coconuts, but still she could not dislodge one. Eventually he picked up a coconut and bent over to give it to the child – whose delight was slightly dampened by the shower she received from Andrew's hat-brim.

Andrew Smith at Petworth fair.

Many a man, when he approaches three score years and ten leaves strife and ambition behind him, in their stead to cultivate a philosophical spirit resigned to waning powers; not Andrew. 'Retirement from work' was an alien concept to him. Travelling was more than his livelihood, it was his life. He travelled in order to earn his bread so that he could travel to earn his bread. He still had wife and daughters completely dependent on him, and after 1914 the family experienced real hardship. War meant the cessation of most fairs and so Andrew resorted to collecting old iron and general dealing to earn a living.

On a long string round his neck he carried different sized saucepan lids for sale and, equipped with seaming-iron, he knocked at doors to enquire, "Any pots or kittles to mend terday?"

He often turned up at Bennyfold Farm, near Petworth.

"Mother, can I have a cabbage?" he'd ask, and was allowed to help himself to as many as he wanted, supplying them in return with a new broom or brush.

His daughter, Rosa, sometimes accompanied him on his calls. She was driving with him through Wisborough Green in May 1916 when they were stopped by a constable. It was after lighting-up time and there was no front lamp or rear red light on their cart. They were fined one shilling for each offence.[20] Not long after this, Andrew was thrown from his cart through the antics of a restive young horse. As a result both his legs were broken. There was nothing for it but a lengthy stay in the Cottage Hospital.[21] By the time Andrew was on his feet again, his family affairs had reached a parlous state. His wife had turned to her usual solace and, after appearing before the Petty Sessions, was fined five shillings for being drunk.[22] Two of his daughters were taken into a local asylum where the weekly cost of their keep was twenty-five shillings. On his return from hospital after Christmas their father was faced with a summons for their maintenance.[23]

Andrew Smith owned a piece of land for which he had paid a hundred pounds and there was a railway carriage and other buildings on it. "He must have money," said the Petworth Board of Guardians. Andrew hobbled into the court, rusty black suit, bowler hat above time-battered face. The land was all mortgaged, he said, and the fairs had stopped because of the War, and he could never earn twenty-five shillings a week by collecting rags and bones. In fact, since the War he hadn't earned as much as a pound a week. He offered to contribute two shillings a week for each daughter and the Justice made an order accordingly.

Downland Post (1 September 1925) published a photograph of Andrew Smith at Ebernoe Fair that summer after he had just traditionally opened proceedings by taking the first 'tuppence' with his shies. Ebernoe's ancient celebration, revived in 1864, had continued to keep its hold on popular imagination. Every year a sheep was roasted whole while a game of cricket was in progress until, at the conclusion of the match, the batsman with the highest score received the animal's horns as trophy. Every year someone would raise the question of the ritual's possible significance. Did Ebernoe's Horn Ceremony contain echoes of primitive tribal initiations or had it originated in the more mundane meeting of the cutlery trade to purchase horns for handles? For country people living locally, however, the significance of the event lay not in the past but in the present. Each year Ebernoe Fair reminded them it was time to sow cabbages, just as at Petworth the annual fair prompted gardeners to sow their broad beans.

In a corner of Andrew's yard at Strood Green an iron rim of a solid wheel stood resting on bricks to provide the hearth. Over the fire was suspended a huge

Andrew Smith at Ebernoe Horn Fair, 1920s.

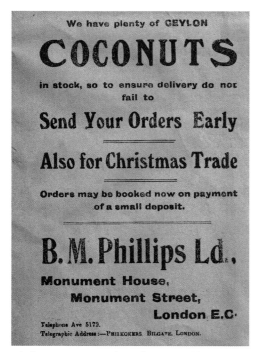

We have plenty of CEYLON

COCONUTS

in stock, so to ensure delivery do not
fail to

Send Your Orders Early

Also for Christmas Trade

Orders may be booked now on payment
of a small deposit.

B. M. Phillips Ld.,

Monument House,
Monument Street,
London E.C.

Telephone Ave 5172.
Telegraphic Address:—Philkokers, Bilgate, London.

Phillips Coconuts advert from *World's Fair*,
4 December 1915.

Brass coconut token quoted with coconut orders as a
guarantee of payment.

cooking-pot inside of which dangled a cluster of nets containing meat, various vegetables and puddings. Beside his wagon he had also by now accumulated a heap of old iron and a collection of animals – chickens, dogs, a large malodorous goat and above all, horses. Andrew loved his horses, and almost one of the family was Billy-Colt, who could always be trusted to deliver him and Amy safely back home from the pub when both were too drunk to drive.

In the summer of 1931 Amy was taken into hospital, but Andrew still went about making his living in the usual way. One very hot morning a local resident was toying with the idea of picking her blackcurrants when she caught sight of his sturdy figure stomping up the garden path with a couple of mats over his arm.

"Any rugs or mats terday, Mother?"

She shook her head, unable to contemplate buying rugs in such hot weather.

"Lovely place you've got here, Mum, and beautiful blackcurrants. Give yer two pun for yer blackcurrants, Mum, if my boys can pick 'em terday."

The woman shook her head again. Andrew, sweat trickling off his chin and his black hair matted under his hat, smiled magnanimously.

"Orl right then. Two pun five fer the currants, and I'll take yer apples come October. Right? They'll be more nor you can want on that tree."

"My fruit is not for sale," the house-dweller said firmly.

Andrew sighed.

"Could I have a drink, Mum?"

"I can give you water or tea. Which would you like?"

"Water, please, Mum. I've summat in my pocket to cheer'un up."

Sitting on the garden seat, he removed his hat and mopped his forehead with a red handkerchief.

Meanwhile, his boys, guarding the cart and ancient horse, awaited him outside. The woman brought a jug of water and three glasses.

"Would your sons like some?"

Andrew pulled a flask from his pocket.

"Thirst does a young 'un good. Teaches 'un a thing or two. But at my age one wants a drop, else one would dry up entirely."

He poured brandy generously into the tumbler of water and tipped the half-pint down his throat. Replacing the glass on the tray, he heaved an immense sigh and closed his eyes. His sons stood motionless by the cart.

"And how is your wife keeping?" the woman asked. Andrew's face clouded.

"My woman's in hospital, Mum. Termorrer I go to

fetch her back home. Doctor, he's good to her, but she's used to a drop of rum in her night tea, an' she doesn't take to a house. Yus, termorrer I fetches her home." He struggled to his feet, made a bow and departed.

The woman happened to meet the doctor next evening and asked: "Has old Andrew fetched his wife from the hospital?"

He nodded.

"He has, although I could have sworn the old girl hadn't the strength to walk across the ward, she climbed up into the cart, and sat bolt upright beside him. She won't last the month, and the rum tea will finish her off a little quicker probably, but they'll be happier. She was like a caged animal; always lived in a tent or a van. Over eighty too, though a mere child compared with Andrew."

"What age is he then?" asked the woman, remembering the olive complexion and black hair.

"Almost a hundred as far as anyone knows. Father was a Romany, they say."

When Andrew's wife died in 1933, their grandson had to come to terms with the idea of human mortality.

Andrew Smith and his grandson at Petworth fair.

"Grandad," he asked, "when are YOU going to die?"

Andrew looked seriously at the lad: "Wal, it's like this. I've grown too tough to die now. I reckon, when my time comes, they're gonner have to shoot me."

Three years later "Ev'ry one a good 'un!" – the familiar cry rang out for the last time at Petworth's November Fair.

West Sussex Gazette (18 March 1937) reported:

DEATH OF ANDREW SMITH – *England's Oldest Travelling Showman*
With his passing West Sussex (and indeed several counties) loses a familiar human landmark ...

The newspaper went on to attribute to the dying man an overwhelming concern for the welfare of the traditional fairs that he had done so much to preserve.

His last words were thanks to the many people who had so loyally supported him at the Charter Fairs, and he expressed the hope that those who follow him on the fairgrounds would do their utmost to keep them open.

The vicar, the Reverend Godrey Wells, conducted his funeral and Kirdford Parish church was filled beyond capacity as travellers arrived from all parts of the country to pay their respects. Partly Andrew's character, partly his lineage, drew them.

"He mightn't have had much money, but look at the respect he's got. Now, that's a sign of back-life,' whispered one mourner.

The year that Andrew died Ebernoe Horn Fair was not a success. Because its statutory date (25 July) fell on a Sunday, it was held on the Saturday before. The resultant confusion meant that hardly any travelling showmen attended. In fact, the only fair folk to turn up were Andrew's son and daughter-in-law, but people were happy to see that they had brought with them the familiar coconut-shy.

'*Greatly missed was the late Andrew Smith, but it was pleasant to find the traditions of so old a family are being maintained*,' reported *West Sussex Gazette*.[24]

Andrew's influence extended beyond his lifetime. He, his children and grandchildren interwove their destinies with other travelling folk, particularly with the Matthews clan. Their future, as it unfolded, bore the equally distinctive mark of Andrew's arch rival, Harelip Matthews.

Andrew Smith. Hammond's juvenile roundabout on left.

Chapter Eight
HARELIP AND MISFORTUNE

Manslaughter – Joseph Matthews, the proprietor of a shooting gallery, was again charged on remand with slaying Phoebe Sarah Jane Matthews at the Odd Fellows' and Foresters' Fête on the 30th ult.

(*West Sussex Gazette*, 24 July 1884)

Harelip was born just before Christmas in 1852 and christened at Shottermill in Surrey on 6 February 1853. Not quite ten years old when his mother died, he never understood why her death left him with such a sense of betrayal. He just remembered how, one moment the whole family had been caught up in the exertions of the 'back end run', a few fairs left before pulling in at Aldershot, excited at new opportunities opening out at the Camp. The next, Liddy was lying sick and dying, something almost mochardi about her death. Harelip couldn't understand it.

When other travellers died, the folk came from far and wide to pay respects. There were great gatherings where everyone talked and talked about the lost one, dwelling on how they'd looked and what they'd said in their last hours. Why hadn't this happened when Liddy died? The only thing folks kept going on about was her weak chest and how it wasn't surprising the bronchitis did for her. Poor Liddy, poor Liddy, they said – before passing to another subject as quickly as if lives depended on it.

At the time of his mother's death the family was travelling a various assortment of sideshows. Harelip's memories reached back to his earlier childhood when he was often put in charge of the 'Knock-'em-downs,' called upon to face the slings and arrows of outraged punters.

Every August Chewbacca liked to attend the 'Sussex Fortnight' of race-meetings at Goodwood, Brighton and Lewes. Corners of the public enclosures were let out to showmen. In 1858 he arrived at Brighton Races with a nicely painted set of 'Dolls', three black dummy heads in the mouths of which were stuck short tobacco pipes. The aim of the game was to knock the pipe out of the mouth of one of the figures from a distance of ten yards by hurling 'livetts' (sticks eighteen inches long and as thick as a man's wrist). Harelip's job was to gather up the livetts after they had been thrown, and proffer them three a penny to potential punters.

A most affable gentleman approached the stall one afternoon and paid for no less than thirty throws in succession, being cheered all the while by a noisy band of supporters.

"Stunner, your Grace!"

"Oh, I say, another rattler!"

Little Harelip, busily dodging back and forth with the livetts, was enjoying the excitement until it came to a premature halt.

The Duke of Beaufort, for such was the name of the determined contestant, was just taking a most killing aim when the horse of a gentleman riding past knocked against him. Intensely irritated, the noble lord turned his fire from the Dolls to the horseman, pouring against his retreating back a rapid cannonade with the sticks still in his hand. A violent altercation ensued until the Duke, taking the law and a leg into his own hand, pushed the rider off his horse. The antagonists glared at each other over the animal's back, just as weeks later they glared at each other in court when both were called to answer a summons for assault.

The many witnesses called to give evidence corroborated each other in most details, especially in the matter of the Duke's skill in playing at Aunt Sally.

"He's a right good 'un at it," a cabman confided to the judge. Notwithstanding, the Duke was found guilty and required to pay a hundred pounds damages. On the other hand, the Duke won his cross-summons, maintaining that the horse brushing against him constituted an assault in law. He was awarded damages assessed at one farthing.[1] A few years later there was further trouble with knock-'em-downs on Brighton Race Course. This time an over-eager contestant hurled a livett with such force that it flew over the canvas protection behind the coconuts and struck a passer-by on the temple, felling him like an ox. The poor fellow was bandaged up and taken away while an official ordered the removal of the game that was proving such a threat to public safety.[2]

On his regular forays into Sussex, Harelip often met up with Jack Harris, a prominent travelling showman based in the Lewes area. Jack's origins are obscure but a story exists that he was a foundling child introduced into the household of the Duchess of Abercorn to earn his keep. In later life he sported her coat of arms on his wesket and on the centre-engine of his roundabout as tribute to this aristo-cratic patronage.

Jack married Matilda Mary Light. On the 1871 Census they are reported living in a caravan in Workhouse Lane, Framfield, together with their eight children who had been born in villages scattered the length and breadth of Sussex.

Name	Relation to head of family	Condition	Age	Occupation	Where born
John Harris	Head	Married	40	Licensed Hawker	Waldron
Mary Matilda	Wife	..	38		Ringmer
Mary Ann	Daughter	Unmarried	17		E. Hothly
Maria	Daughter	..	15		Hellingly
Celia	Daughter	..	12		Lindfield
Edward	Son	..	10		Keymer
Frederick	Son	..	8		Chalvington
Clara	Daughter	..	6		Lindfield
Moses	Son	..	4		Wivelsfield
Louisa	Daughter	..	2		Lower Beeding

Flash Ria, Harelip's wife.

It is not known when Jack's second daughter, Maria, became the special object of Harelip's attention, but he had left his own clan to join forces with hers by the beginning of 1875. In February of that year the law recorded his presence on the Harrises' terrain by fining him one shilling for allowing his horses to stray on the highway at Piddinghoe, near Lewes.[3]

Maria (or Ria, as she was generally called) would have held an immediate attraction for any young man of spirit. Her tall erect figure and flashing dark eyes commanded attention; her crowning glory black tresses never washed but kept clean and shiny by frequent applications of coconut oil. Dressed in bright-coloured pinafore, she marched with a red flag into towns to warn of the approach of her father's steam road locomotive.

She was very proud of her appearance, rejoicing in the acquisition of new clothes, if not always brave enough to wear them. Her father was the problem. He disapproved of her extravagance and her taste, so, more often than not, Ria's new clothes had to be stuffed in a sack under the bed so that Jack would not see them. When she made the mistake of trying to keep the affairs of her heart similarly in the dark, the consequences were severe. Inevitably Jack found out that his daughter was being courted behind his back and he exploded with rage, taking off his belt and whipping her in front of the family. Ria never forgave him for the humiliation and the loss of her first suitor, although publicly she declared:

"I don't care what Father says, I'm gonner marry the next fella who asks me."

And this is how Flash Ria came to link her fortunes with Harelip, an otherwise unlikely candidate for her affections. Below average height, his figure stubby, his temperament stubborn. Then there was his disfigured mouth and voice so mangled you hardly bothered to listen to the words but looked to his eyes and fists to know what he was saying. And yet, for good or ill, the match was made and both stayed the rough course for nearly half a century.

The young couple spent their first years travelling with the bride's family. At Lamb Fair in Horsham in 1875 Harelip's father-in-law, described as 'a coconut man', was charged with being drunk. He was fined five shillings, and paid up happily, confessing as he did so that he had come to court expecting to be charged with assault as well.[4]

The following year Ria gave birth to a son, named for his father, Joseph. He was born on 11 January near Heathfield, Sussex, where they had spent the winter, and christened at Waldron on 23 January 1876. Harelip waited another few weeks before joining the Harrises on the road. Their circuit covered Sussex, parts of Kent and Hampshire. As summer drew on the pace was terrific.

'Singing Charley Lee', travelling with the same outfit, later recalled:

'I was with J. Harris when he had his first set of gallopers, which was the only machine of that class travelling Sussex, also parts of Kent and Hants, at that period. Our winter quarters were at Burgess Hill, Sussex, or Lewes.

'Mind you, in those days it was all 'go', club hunting and Fair keeping. I am going back to the 80s when the Club feast days were all the go. Whitsun week was a killer in those times – six gaffs that week – pretty good going! Tunbridge Wells Common, Whit Monday; pull down and on to Rushlake Green for Tuesday, Crowborough Club on Wednesday; Glynde Club on Thursday; and Blackboys Club on Friday. Then on to Uckfield in the Bell Brook fair ground for our Saturday night, and six of us used to pull those gallopers down and have them loaded and ready for the road in two and a half hours. It was a Walker machine from Tewkesbury, a 14 swift lot with 36 horses and two boats, but after a few years Harris had a new centre and Savages altered the machine into a 12 swift lot which did away with the two boats. But it was still driven by the Walker engine and a brass plate on the centre engine had "*Morning Star*" engraved on it.

'… I recall one occasion many years ago when we were built up at a big temperance fête in a park at Tunbridge Wells. The brass trumpet organ was in its infancy, long before the paper organ made its debut. Ours was a Chiappi organ and it played one tune that was quite a rage in those times, "*Beer, Beer, Glorious Beer*." Old man Harris impressed on me to miss this tune for that day, but when we got busy riding I changed the tune and, not noticing it, I gave them "*Beer, Beer*" for about an hour or so. The local papers had it in big print the next morning: "Beer in plenty at a temperance fête!"

'They were strenuous times then; there was no system like they have now. It was first come, first served for the tober and devil take the hindmost. I recall seeing many a good old rough and tumble fight over the ground. Still that was all in the game those days, and soon forgotten.'[5]

'Singing Charley Lee' was a pseudonym for Charles William Wickenden, born in Rottingdean in 1872, son of a coastguard officer. He had a fine alto voice and as a boy sang in the local church choir. At sixteen Charley left home on foot, only a few bob in his pocket and no idea what he was going to do. By evening he had reached Henfield and, feeling very sorry for himself, went into a pub for some bread and cheese and a pint. There was a gang of high-spirited young men in the bar who all spoke to Charley quite cheerfully. A good crowd, he thought. They were arguing over the words of a popular song, and after Charley repeated it for them, they asked if he would sing it. This he did, much to their delight. After this they bought him a drink, asked where he came from and listened while he explained how he had left home and was looking for work. The people he was talking to were Ria's brothers, Chris and Reuben Harris, and some of the chaps.

'Why not come with our lot?' they said. 'We'll see the old man and get you in; we could do with another chap.'

Next morning Chris and Reuben took him to their Dad, old Jack Harris, and he started him on a life that Charley took to as if to the manner born.

Soon Chris and Reuben were telling people from other outfits, 'We gotta chap with us that will sing anything you like, he knows 'em all.' Hence the name 'Singing Charley.' After staying years with Harrises, he travelled with Mrs Pettigrove, then with Hastings and Whayman's switchback before finishing his travelling days with 'Rocky' Tom Andrews' gallopers of Tunbridge Wells. In 1903 he married Olive Ripley who came from a travelling family, and they spent the first years of their married life in Highbrooms, Kent.

At the back end of the year showmen journeyed into Hampshire for one of the oldest fairs in England,

Pettigrove's steam switchback at Lindfield fair, 1922.

Charley and Olive, taken at Lewes Road, Brighton, 1917. The family always referred to Charlie's trousers as: 'the old man's dordy twilers'.

held at Weyhill on Old Michaelmas Day, 10 October. Sited at the crossing point of the Tin Road from Cornwall and the Gold Road from Wales, and close to a Bronze Age barrow, its ancient origins were manifest. In the 1870s the Horning of the Colts ceremony was still being enacted on the eve of the fair. All young men attending for the first time were crowned with a pair of horns between which a cup of ale had been fixed. After the old-timers had sung several choruses of:

So swiftly runs the hare, so cunning runs the fox,
Why shouldn't this young calf grow up to be an
  ox?
And get his living among the briars and thorns,
And die like his daddy with a long pair of horns,

the newcomer quaffed the ale and then bought a further half-gallon to be shared with the company.

Harelip and his brother John had a thirst on them that required no such excuse for the quenching. They were both at Weyhill in 1877. The fair lasted ten days, and their wives took advantage of the lengthy stay to take their newborn infants into St Michael's church for christening. The Parish Register records the baptism of John, son of Joseph and Maria Matthews, whose normal abode was Lewes, although then attending Weyhill Fair as 'hawkers'.

A year later Ria and Harelip carried their third son into Weyhill Church, and asked for him to be christened Jemmy. The little lad was ailing. It was a wonder he had survived so long. Immediately after his birth four weeks previously Harelip had fetched the minister of Cuckfield and brought him up into the wagon to baptise the baby. Ria was not at all sure the ritual had been sufficient, so now she brought Jemmy to church to have the service done 'properly'. Maybe she even hoped to effect a cure and found it hard to forgive the Almighty when four months later the little chavvy, despite all her care, passed from her. The only consolation was that there was no quibbling when it came to giving the child decent Christian burial. For this reason travellers were meticulous about having all their babies baptised.

The country was in the throes of agricultural depression. Teg Fair, April 1879, was the largest but dullest ever seen at Horsham. Not surprisingly, therefore, at Loxwood Show the following month the toasts were full of references to hard times. It was only in the accompanying pleasure fair amid the excitement of coconut shies, roundabouts and gingerbread stalls, that the English farmer forgot his troubles. The showmen took a lot of 'dosh' and the only man not doing good business was the recruiting sergeant trying to enlist young fellows to fight the Zulus.[6]

In the second week of June Harelip was caught 'poovin the grais' again – this time at Linch where two of his horses were feeding off the wayside. With philosophical resignation he called at the police station leaving a sovereign to cover the costs. In due course the magistrates imposed a fine of fourteen shillings and directed that the miscreant be given six shillings change if his whereabouts could be discovered.[7] It seems he was being allowed liberal discount for cash. When, a week later, Jack Harris was charged with a similar offence he had to pay one pound plus costs.[8] Harelip built up his shooting-gallery in the Market Square, Petersfield, for the Town Fair in July before moving to Passfield for the Club Feast. At Bramshott he was involved in a fracas started by his brother Chorley, and just managed to escape another fine.[9] Were the authorities now on the lookout for him? Early in the following season they summoned him for allowing horses to stray on the highway leading from East Meon to Privett. This time Harelip decided to keep them waiting for the fine of eleven shillings and sixpence.[10]

Ria gave birth to their third surviving son, William, in October 1880. Ten days before Christmas Harelip set out before dawn, taking with him his nifty jukel, Toby. He met up with his two pals who had a cart, and the three men drove towards Midhurst. By mid-morning they had managed to acquire a load of holly, and after a convivial drink at the *Jolly Drovers* made their way homeward.

It was while they were driving across Terwick Common that they spotted the hare. Now, Harelip's dog was in need of a bit of exercise so was not restrained when it leapt from the cart to give tongue and chase. He caught it, and so did his master ... when a constable suddenly materialised from the hedgerow.

"A hare? What do yer mean? We don't know nuffin abart any 'are."

And the three men looked suitably amazed when the constable uncovered the still-warm corpse on their cart.

"Oh, that one," said Harelip's pal brightly. "I jus' picked that up orf the road back there."

When the three were each fined one pound for poaching Harelip produced a handful of sovereigns in court and disdainfully paid the lot.

Not long after this the dog became a bone of contention. Often he went missing only to turn up again hours later with a furry or feathery souvenir of his excursion, but just before Easter 1881 Toby disappeared for weeks. When Harelip set eyes on his prized jukel next, it was being let off a rope held by James Pocock, colt-breaker of Petersfield. A fierce argument ensued.

"It's my dog, I tell you. I bought him fair and aboveboard from a man in the pub: and that was months since," said Pocock.

Repartee was not Harelip's strong point; he quickly tired of verbal exchange.

"It's mine," he stated doggedly before picking Toby up and walking off with him. An hour later saw Pocock, accompanied by a policeman, knocking on the door of Harelip's wagon parked in Petersfield Square.

"Mr Matthews? I've had a complaint from this gentleman that you just snatched his dog ..." The one-sided debate recommenced. Harelip listened passively as Pocock's story of legitimate purchase was repeated. Toby was picked up and carried away in the arms of the law.

Following the constable at a discreet distance, Harelip watched him hand the dog to Pocock and take his leave. Pocock put the animal on the ground. Harelip swooped and made off with Toby again.

Magistrates listened to the tale with mounting bewilderment before deciding that they had no power to interfere between a man and his dog. They suggested the protagonists sort out their dispute in a civil court. It didn't come to that; what Harelip had, he held on to.[11]

On the 1881 Census Harelip and his family are found living at Lion Green in Frensham, Surrey, together with their three sons, Harelip's father, and one servant.

Name	Relation to head of family	Condition	Age	Occupation	Where born
Joseph Matthews	head	married	25	Hawker, employing one man	Hindhead, Sy
Maria ..	wife	..	23		Chotingly, Sx
Joseph ..	son	unmarried	5		Crossinghand, Sx
John ..	son	..	4		North Camp, Sy
William ..	son	..	5 months		Guildford, Sy
James ..	father	widower	75		Chidingley, Sx
Robert Davis	servant	unmarried	23		Dorchester, Dorset

Life with old Chewbacca, however, was never without its problems and at Guildford Court of Petty Sessions in July 1883 the magistrates were treated to a pretty tale of strife. It seemed that Harelip's father, described unflatteringly as 'a drunken old vagabond' had insulted Betsy Smith, hawker. Betsy had picked up a 'roley-poley', a stick used to place the coconuts on, and struck him in the eye, at the same time belabouring him with disgraceful language. According to Betsy, what happened next was that Harelip, without a word, came up to her, hit her in the face with his fist and knocked her unconscious. Harelip denied the charge and Chewbacca appeared as witness to explain that his poor son was not even present at the time of the incident 'as he had gone to buy a horse.' Consequently, the defendant was discharged. In a separate case Betsy was fined one pound for assaulting the old man.[12]

Harelip and Ria were at this time travelling the fairs with swing boats and shooting-gallery, their eldest chavvy, Joe, aged eight, working manfully at his father's side. Ria liked to be taking the money when the stuff was open, but her hands were often full with looking after the babies who arrived at regular two-year intervals. Her first daughter, Annie, had been born in August 1882, and then in early summer 1884 there was another boy. He was christened Henry.

When they arrived at Petersfield on 30 June 1884 to open at the Odd Fellows' and Foresters' Fête there was no sign that a scene was being set for tragedy.[13] There was the usual frantic bustle of activity as the loads pulled into the field and the rides and sidestuff were built up. The event was an annual engagement for Harelip and his brother Chorley, and both their families looked forward to it. As long as the weather held fine local people would flock to enjoy their Club Day; holiday mood making for heedless spending. It was happy money the showmen took at village clubs.

And then, in the course of the afternoon when the party food was handed out, the showmen's chavvies were generously included in the distribution.

Chorley's second daughter, Carrie, had died of scarlet fever at Horsham Fair almost exactly ten years previously. His family now comprised seven children ranging from Lydia, sixteen, down to the baby of the family, Janie, aged four. When this little one was given a slice of pudding by the Club organisers, she clambered up on to a chair behind the side-stuff with her plate in one hand and sat munching the delicious treat.

Meanwhile, two gentlemen had approached Harelip's shooting-gallery. One of them was an expert marksman. His bullet hit the bull's-eye, passed right through the back of the gallery and lodged in Janie's head. The child died three hours later.

Naturally, no blame attached to the marksman, but once it was shown that the bull's-eye plate was defective, the proprietor of the gallery was found guilty of manslaughter by a coroner's jury. Harelip was committed for trial at the next County Assizes, but admitted to bail in his own recognizance for forty pounds and one surety in a like amount. After that he had to wait for over a month for the case to be heard. The intervening weeks were hell.

Nearly all travellers love chavvies. Turbulent, often violent people though they were, the toughest among them responded like a shepherd before the Babe when a chavvy was hurt. Now, one of the dearest of their little ones lay dead. The family, the whole clan, grieved. Harelip grieved, and would never stop grieving. At the same time there was that other world with its flatties' system of justice accusing Harelip of a monstrous crime.

'They' called down experts from London gunsmiths. 'They' examined witnesses. 'They' questioned Harelip again and again. Who erected the gallery? Did he check the bullet-box? What condition was the bell-clapper in? And, it didn't matter what answers he gave, still the little chavvy lay dead and nothing could bring her back.

Harelip waited in dumb misery for his trial. At last the day came. The courtroom was crowded with travellers, his brothers' and sisters' families, his uncles and cousins, all come to support the accused. Then the judge stopped the case almost before it started, stating that evidence showed the killing to be purely an accident. The prisoner was discharged – to serve a self-imposed life-sentence.

Harelip and Chorley had always been close, often travelling together to the same gaffs for a season. Just weeks before the tragedy, when Ria was having a hard time in childbirth, it was Chorley's wife Phoebe who delivered the chavvy into the world. Ria was feeding little Henry when the men rushed up to the wagons shouting crazily that a chavvy had been shot and was mullerin on the ground. For minutes she had no way of telling whose chavvy had been hurt. Then she saw the crowd pass by to Phoebe's wagon and Chorley carrying the pitiful bundle and she knew it was Janie. She groaned and clutched her own baby closer to her. Henry set up a reproachful wail.

It was August before the manslaughter charge against Harelip was dropped. Grief, shock and anxiety took their toll. In the following month there was trouble at Rogate Fair when Ria ran amok.[14] She had been drinking, heavily, in the bar of the *White Horse*. One of the travellers said something tactless and Ria exploded. During the chaos that ensued she smashed her right hand through a window. Police Sergeant Read appeared on the scene and spoke to the distraught woman. He possibly chose the wrong words. Ria struck him in the face, smothering it with her own blood. She pummelled him in the chest as he dragged her from the bar. Other women intervened, catching hold of the wit-crazed woman and hustling her into her husband's wagon to calm down.

Ten minutes later out she came again. Flew up the street to the police sergeant, straight in once more with her right fist.

"Lock me up; I want to be locked up," she demanded.

Ria was convicted of assault, but got off with a surprisingly light fine, the police disinclined to keep this screaming virago behind bars.

'Flash Ria' with her high and mighty ways was not popular with other travelling women, but now they tried to talk sense into her.

"Yer can't afford for ter let yerself go like this, not with them dear little chavvies of yourn needin' yer. Your goin' on like a dinilow don't help Phoebe none, and it's her as got cause for grievin'. You jus' oughter be thinkin' of yer own chavvies and be thankful they's alright."

After the back-end run Chorley went back to his piece of land in Headley while Harelip pulled into a yard at Haslemere which was becoming his regular winter quarters. He suffered a further blow when his brother Johnny died at Weyhill Fair in October 1885. The breath of the Mulo-mush was still hanging heavily over the family at Christmas. To shake it off Harelip made preparations to take to the road early in 1886. Then Henry, the baby, fell ill, and within a week had died of meningitis.

Harelip felt himself enmeshed in misfortune. He had got rid of the shooting-gallery immediately after Janie's death, vowing never to have anything to do with guns again. Occasionally, however, he went back to provide 'all the fun of the fair' in the neighbourhood where she was killed. It took little to stir dark emotions in such a setting. On the third anniversary of the tragedy, at the place where it happened, one Frederick Stacey, fishmonger of Petersfield, said the wrong thing and Harelip knocked him to the ground.[15] Harelip was thirty-five. There was a lot of fight left in him yet.

Chapter Nine
BATTLE FOR PITCHES

Chichester County Bench
Rival Showmen at Selsey Club

Matthews, senior, took off his jacket and waistcoat and wanted Smith to fight,
but Smith declined. There has been previous conduct of this kind, and the defendants
had avowed the intention of frightening complainants from the district.
(*West Sussex Gazette*, 19 June 1902)

Ownership of a steam roundabout had elevated Redshirt in the fairground hierarchy. Not only was he doing well for himself, he was flash with it. Nothing galled Harelip more than to see his brother lording it over other showmen when they met up at annual gaffs such as Petworth.

'Matthews' Merry go round, evidently the attraction of the fair, was started at eleven o'clock in the morning and kept going till nearly midnight. During nearly all this time it was well patronised and the proprietor must have done very good business,' commented a local news reporter in 1888, clearly impressed.[1] Harelip, waiting to help people to mount, two at a time, into his swing-boats, stared stonily at Redshirt's crowded machine.

Other showmen were soon stealing a march on Harelip, too. Ria's father, Jack Harris, had invested in his smart set of steam gallopers manufactured by Walkers of Tewkesbury and although it took six men two and a half hours to pull them down, pack them up and have them ready for the road – and at the other end the next build-up – there were certain rewards. For, picked out in gold scroll on the rounding-board, revolving as the horses rose and fell, the proprietor's name would proclaim his achievement. By definition the proprietor of a steam-roundabout was a man of substance. Ria was very conscious of such things.

All Petworth was *en fête* in July 1890 for the coming of age of Lord Leconfield's heir. House-dwellers hung

Harris's steam gallopers at Lewes Sheep Fair, 1891.

Chinese lanterns in the streets; one lady placing at intervals round every window in front of her house scores of lights in small coloured glasses. In Petworth Park more than three thousand cottagers and their families sat down in huge marquees to enjoy a meat tea whilst regaled by the Band of the British Orchestra.

'Then there was Harris's Royal Steam Riding Circus, which was kept going till 8 p.m. to the amusement of the hundreds of young folk, and we may say elderly ones too, while near the roundabout were swing boats and shying for coconuts, and the variety entertainment which took place on the stage from half-past four till eight.'[2] Harris's 'Steam Riding Circus' – the name was cannily chosen. Jack knew that proprietors of travelling 'circuses' could take advantage of concessionary railway rates not available to ordinary fairground travellers.

Ria was impressed by her father's machine and started to cajole Harelip. Their fourth surviving son, Moses, was born in 1891. The future was with them. They pulled the bag of sovereigns from under the bed and made their decision. They had enough for a down-payment on a steam-roundabout, one that would be possibly – no, definitely – bigger and grander than Harris's and Redshirt's.

Off Harelip set for King's Lynn, where the following entry soon appeared in Savage's Order Book:

DATE:	1892
NO:	551
DESCRIPTION:	Make 1 double cylinder engine No 5½
SOLD TO:	Matthews

DATE:	1892
NO:	550
DESCRIPTION:	Make 1 No. 3 organ engine
SOLD TO:	Matthews

At Littlehampton the following Whit Monday from an early hour until quite late at night a steam roundabout of gigantic proportions with galloping horses was in motion on the common, and as the evening drew on was brilliantly illuminated by electricity.[3]

They had achieved their ambition by entering the select circle of steam roundabout proprietors – but other travellers still found fault, nagged at them to climb a further step towards conventional respectability. After all, Ria had borne nine children during the twenty years they had been together. Time surely to regularise the situation.

Harelip's 'Royal Steam Galloping Horses' at Chichester Sloe fair in 1890s.

Showmen's living-wagons at Sloe Fair in 1890s.

Ria seized the opportunity to buy a new outfit – a long-skirted costume with matching hat and parasol in her favourite colour, heliotrope, and on 13 January 1894 their marriage was solemnized at St Pancras Church, Chichester, with Fred and Betsy Harris standing as witnesses.

Now Harelip set about consolidating his professional life. Not all grounds were big enough to take two steam roundabouts. He had to work hard to secure a run of tobers to accommodate the new machine, taking care not to clash with the Harrises on tour. To draw the heavier loads he bought a Burrell road locomotive (8 n.h.p. No. 1628) and was promptly fined ten shillings in September 1893 for using it at Lindfield without a licence.[4] Horses, nevertheless, were still Harelip's mainstay on the road, and he was continually in trouble over these, too. Being fined for allowing horses to stray on public highways he regarded as an occupational hazard and usually paid up without argument. He did not show such forbearance when summoned for furious driving and using obscene language at Storrington in May 1895. In court a police constable testified that Harelip's horse had galloped through the town at between twelve and fifteen miles per hour, with people having to stand in the water table to get out of the rider's way. Harelip patiently explained that he had been doing his best to restrain the beast that was running away with him at the time. The court, unimpressed, fined him ten shillings.[5]

Littlehampton May Fair, at which Matthews' Monster Roundabout had been chief attraction the previous year, came under attack in 1895. The urban district council despatched a memorial to Mr Asquith requesting its abolition because of the nuisance caused to townsfolk when their main streets were obstructed. The Home Secretary must have been bemused to receive soon afterwards a counter-petition signed by nearly every resident in Surrey Street, where the fair was held, for its retention. After due consideration he announced that there did not seem to be clear grounds for his interference in the matter.[6]

Town officials disliked charter fairs so often bringing confusion and mayhem into their nicely organised streets and were determined to be rid of them. As a result, showmen were finding themselves at war with society on several fronts. It was not just their livelihood, but their whole way of life that was being challenged by the proliferation of committees concerned with housing, sanitation and health regulations. In Brighton in 1886 the town council was urged to limit the number of occupants in each caravan standing in Islingword Road to one, because of insufficient air-space in each at night.[7] But it was not suffocation which caused the death of three year old Polly Whitehead in her parents' house-cart at Horsham the following month. The little girl had swallowed a bone while eating her supper. Her father rushed her to a doctor who agreed to operate, but there was a snag. The operation must be done in hospital and the workhouse hospital would not admit the child on her own. It would be necessary first for both her parents to surrender their wagon and sign themselves into the workhouse from which there would be little hope of escape to any future independence.

"You want us to make paupers of ourselves?" the father cried in disbelief. The answer was uncompromising. There was no certainty the child's life could be saved, so he took his little girl back to the wagon where she died in her mother's arms.[8] Behind this increasing pressure on the travellers' way of life was a political campaign mounted by George Smith M.P. who in 1889 brought a Private Member's Bill before the House of Commons to ensure that all living-vans were registered every three years and inspected. Children, too, were to be registered and attend school regularly. Showmen recognised the threat inherent in such legislation and joined forces to defeat it. They formed the United Kingdom Showmen and Van Dwellers' Association (U.K.S.V.D.A.).

Doubtless, the proposed Bill was well-intentioned. It even appeared to be wise. In effect, such interference led to absurdities. In 1891 two gypsies were summoned at Dorking for allowing their caravans to be overcrowded in a manner injurious to health. Two parents and two children inhabited each caravan. Each caravan allowing for bedding and furniture, had about 250 cubic feet. A medical officer of health testified that 300 cubic feet was considered the minimum for one adult.

"Surely there would be more ventilation in a van in the open than in a house?" the Chairman of the Bench sensibly asked, before going on to point out that in army camps and prisons the government itself broke the law constantly. The summons was dismissed.

John Smith and his mother slept in a bender-tent of the kind the old lady had lived in all her life. They were visited by the same agent of the Dorking Rural Sanitary Authority on New Year's Eve 1891. The tent's air-space was calculated as 250 cubic feet, and its owner was prosecuted for failing to fit proper flooring. Smith's protestation that "everything in my tent is clean and wholesome" was deemed irrelevant.[9] Yet, had the inspector probed, he would have been amazed at the fastidious hygiene lore inherited, and adhered to, by the travellers.

After five years of campaigning the showmen were rewarded by the defeat of George Smith's Bill. The struggle taught them lessons. They realised what could be achieved if they worked together against forces traditionally opposed to their interests. A new self-image emerged in the course of the conflict. They began to see themselves as respectable businessmen, amusement caterers, proprietors of machines, not on any account to be confused with gypsies, hawkers or pedlars.

Harelip was gratified to hear himself officially described as 'a steam roundabout proprietor' in his court appearances. He paid a fine for two aggravated assaults in Dorking in 1898[10] without demur, but when he came before magistrates in Worthing the following year his indignation knew no bounds. A *gypsy*? Had he heard himself described as a *gypsy*? These flatties were dinilow if they couldn't tell a showman from a gypsy! And surely it must make a difference to the verdict if they knew just what sort of man they were dealing with. He instructed his solicitor to apply for a new trial in the action brought against him to recover £10.15s. for putting his horses in a field belonging to Mr Robinson at East Worthing.

"In the course of his remarks," the solicitor said, "his Honour had referred to Mr Matthews as a 'gypsy' whereas he was not one of that tribe at all but a respectable and prosperous roundabout proprietor, earning more money than a good many gentlemen in the court that morning."

His Honour, however, refused to reconsider, remarking that he had done his best to try the case fairly and without the slightest prejudice.[11]

"Fairs are no longer as they were fifty years ago when country produce was sold and agricultural servants were engaged," said the Chairman of Bognor Council in 1899. The Fair held in the town centre had now increased to four or five days, and closed at twelve o'clock at night, during which time it provided 'music of a hideous nature'. The Clerk said the fair was not held by statute but by an individual in her own field; the Home Secretary would have stopped it as at Horsham if the fair had been held in the street.[12]

Chichester was making a bye-law forbidding the playing of any steam organ to the annoyance of residents or passengers in 'any highway road, lane, footway, square, court, alley or passage ... or any land adjoining or near thereto.' Shooting-galleries, swing boats and roundabouts were also prohibited.[13] An amendment to the new bye-law made an exception of Sloe Fair.[14]

A showman of sensitive disposition might have felt that his presence was not always properly appreciated. At Crawley Fair, 1900, Jack Harris was fined for blocking up the High Street for two hours with two traction engines and fifteen vans. After the build-up, his son had a difference of opinion with the owner of the *George Hotel*, who objected to smoke billowing into his hotel windows while Harris was 'firing up' for the electric light for the roundabouts. Christopher Harris politely listened to the man's objections, and then thumped him. Another summons for assault followed.[15]

No-one objected to Littlehampton Fair on 26 May 1900, because it coincided with general celebrations for the relief of Mafeking. Half-penny squirts and confetti were used with alarming effect and many old scores were paid off with interest. The big success story, however, related to the Aunt Sally stalls where

Bartlett's two Burrell engines: *Pride of the South* (left) and *Majestic* with their three abreast gallopers, the talk of Sloe Fair in 1893 because so beautifully illuminated by electric lights.

targets representing Kruger, Steyn, Viljoen and company took remorseless battering.[16]

Three weeks later Harelip pulled onto the common at Stedham. The manor-reeve reported him and he was summonsed for trespass. Harelip could not let him get away with that. On the night of Stedham Fair he sought out the reeve with the summons in his hand. "It's all through you I've got this," he seethed, poking his elbow into the man's side and treading on his toes.[17] So, Harelip discovered, you didn't even have to hit a man to be fined for assault.

In 1901 Littlehampton's annual fair fell on Whit Monday, so again there was special cause for celebration. Bright sunny weather brought day-excursionists in their hundreds, arriving in town by rail and by sea on the steamboat *The Princess May*.[18] Petersfield Fair at the beginning of October drew the largest collection of amusements seen on the Heath for many years.[19] Winchester Sheep Fair attracted more showmen than usual with its removal from the Broadway to Bar End. Six roundabouts and a switchback attended.

Smith's swing-boats at Littlehampton Fair – Chorley in bowler hat at right.

'Thousands patronised the fair, which at night was a picture of dazzling brilliancy though the discordant sounds of a half-dozen organs grinding against each other was not altogether pleasing to the ear.'[20]

There was the rub! So much competition suddenly in the business. Young Dicky Wall had acquired his splendid Savage's roundabout by 1901 and, having been chastised by his father-in-law Redshirt for his effrontery, went south to establish a fresh territory for himself. Soon he was in conflict with Harelip and a pitched battle on the Hants-Sussex border was narrowly averted.

Trouble arose from the fact that there was hardly any formal letting out of ground to showmen in those days. Being a case of 'First come, first served', the

situation often degenerated to 'Might is Right'. Harelip's chief rival when it came to claiming pitches at regular fairs in Sussex was Andrew Smith.

Smiths, like the Harrises and Walls, through the years had much intermarried with Matthewses with the consequence that their territorial jealousies became spiced with family feuds. Feuding was one of the few luxuries a traveller never denied himself. True, if there was a battle on hand with gorgies, all travellers were as one. But once that battle was over, more lasting excitement was generated by internecine strife. Clan fought clan, family fought family, brother fought brother or sister, father fought son, and husband fought wife. When it came to feuding, a man's loyalty sometimes stretched no further than his fists.

In 1902 Andrew Smith was determined to stake a claim good and early at Selsey Club to be held on Tuesday, 10 June, and so he arrived with his swings and sideshows on the previous Sunday. On Tuesday morning the Matthewses, father and son, appeared on the scene. When Harelip took in the situation, his response was typical. He stripped off his jacket and weskot and challenged Andrew to fight. Strangely, in view of Andrew's fighting reputation, the offer was declined. The reason soon became clear. Having been caught so often on the defensive, Andrew had just begun to realise that he too could lean back on the law. He drove off into Chichester to take out a summons against the Matthewses to show cause why they should not provide sureties to keep the peace. Later, in the magistrates' court, Harelip listened with astonishment as Andrew was described as 'a man well-known in the district who bore an excellent character', while Constable Avis went so far as to testify to the fact that the complainant was a peaceable man. As a result of this legal shamanism Harelip was bound over to keep the peace for six months in the sum of ten pounds.[21]

Within a month the situation was repeated at Lodsworth Club. Harelip, having just been bound over, had to stay out of the ring, but Ria and his sons upheld family honour. A glorious fracas ensued, and Andrew went rushing off again to the courts for legal redress. He took out summonses against Joe and John Matthews, who were accused of continually annoying and threatening the Smiths with the avowed object of forcing them to leave the district.

This time, however, the Matthews' brothers had taken out cross-summonses against Andrew and Joseph Smith. To complete the family party Andrew's wife also summonsed Ria Matthews. The cases against the men were taken first and the evidence given on both sides led the Bench to conclude that their best course was to bind all the parties over, which they did, each in one hundred pounds, with one surety in ten pounds, to keep the peace for six months. The case between the women was then withdrawn.[22]

Leaning back on the law had suddenly lost its appeal. Not only was it expensive, there was no point in fighting a battle in a way that produced no winners, so the bitter wrangling settled back into more traditional moulds.

Andrew Smith officially booked his pitch from the parish council at Wisborough Green Fair for 20 September. Learning their lesson from Selsey Club, Harelip and Ria moved their stuff surreptitiously onto the ground at half-past eleven the night before the fair and when, next morning, they were requested to move to another spot, they refused, putting the parish council at defiance. They were charged with contravening the bye-laws and damaging the recreation ground. Harelip was let off lightly with a fine of £1.10s. but cautioned that if a similar case arose another year the maximum fine would be imposed.[23]

It was about this time that Harelip purchased a piece of land near the railway line in West Worthing to use as his winter quarters. One of his first gaffs each season was Easter Fair at nearby Broadwater Green. For years and years past he had been accustomed to pull on to the site on Good Friday. However, in common with many other boroughs the Worthing corporation was strengthening their control over public amenities such as recreation grounds. Harelip saw this as wanton interference with his traditional rights. The fact that the interference came from duly elected representatives of the local people was irrelevant to him. After all, not being part of the sedentary population, his interests were not represented in these local bodies. His way of life might seem an anomaly to house-dwellers, but it was all he himself knew and it had the virtue of all the lives of his ancestors behind it. When, for any reason, a traveller settled down and took to living in a house, he was not admired by his own kind. Bonds of blood and affection remained, but he was referred to with disdain as having become a 'flattie'. Settling down was regarded as weakness.

At Broadwater on Good Friday, 1902, the showmen were met by officials informing them that the Green was now out of bounds for travelling fairs. Harelip and his son, Joe, treated the news with contempt. They pulled on to the Green, built up their roundabout, swings and stalls, and defied the corporation. After taking legal advice, the corporation drew up new bye-laws to prevent any repetition of the scene.

The following Easter posts and ropes were erected around Broadwater Green. When the showmen arrived on Good Friday a policeman was there to greet them. Pointing to the posts, he explained the showmen were no longer allowed to occupy the usual ground. Harelip nodded his head and said slowly, "I see." It was too late to find another tober for Easter, one of the most important weekends of the year for showmen, marking as it did the end of lean winter months. He climbed on to his traction engine and drove it straight through the posts and ropes. Together with his sons he built up the stuff and opened for business as usual. Harelip had won another round.

No self-respecting corporation could let the matter slide. Within months they had drawn up even more elaborate bye-laws and Councillor Ewen Smith declared that in future, if ANYTHING was done on the green which ought not to be done, then it would be a great surprise to him![24] Whether or not he was disappointed in his prophecy, the new bye-laws certainly dealt a death blow to the old Broadwater Green Easter Fair.

Wickham Fair in Hampshire was under similar threat. It had been held from time immemorial on May 20, but early in 1902 an attempt was made to ban it because of the smallpox epidemic. So strong was local opposition that Fareham Urban District Council had to relent. On Whit Tuesday, after Mr Stubbs had conducted a successful livestock sale, the pleasure fair opened according to custom with the Square crowded with roundabouts and sideshows.[25]

Nevertheless, there were so many new bye-laws it was difficult for a traveller not to transgress as he went about his daily business. At half-past eight on an August evening in 1900 Jack Harris was driving his road locomotive *Masterpiece* (Burrell 8 nhp. No. 1674) down Broadwater Street, Worthing, when suddenly challenged by a policeman. The flare lamp he was using was not good enough. The law required a locomotive to have two efficient lights on the front. Jack was charged also with using four loaded wagons without consent, with not having a red light on the last such wagon, and for using the locomotive in West Sussex when it was licensed only for East Sussex. He was fined ten shillings plus costs for each offence.[26] In 1903 Dicky Wall was stopped at Ball's Hut, Arundel, because his locomotive was pulling four loaded wagons. It was permissible to pull four trucks if one was a water-dandy, but Dicky had put a sleeping wagon at the rear in place of the dandy.

"I've travelled like this to fairs at Petersfield, Chichester, Reading and all through London without any trouble," he maintained in court. "What's more, I've got permission now from the Clerk of the Sussex

Wickham Fair c1900.

County Council in Lewes." The case against him was dismissed.[27]

The 'gavvers' could get at showmen for using a locomotive which did not consume its own smoke, for parking on a drain cover, for obstructing the highway, and for speeding. After Sloe Fair in Chichester in 1907 a traction engine, trying to imagine itself a motor-car, went thundering through Orchard Street at between six and seven miles an hour. Its owner was fined five pounds for fast driving.[28]

Apart from heaviest loads, Harelip still depended for transport on his horses and these were always a liability with regard to the law. When the family was on the move there was the constant problem of finding adequate grazing. 'Poovin the grais' or allowing their horses to stray on the public highway were possible solutions. Horse-drawn vehicles had also to be supplied with adequate lighting when driven in the dark. Harelip's daughter was fined ten shillings for driving her cart without a lamp on the Worthing Road, Littlehampton, in March 1904, and it really wasn't her fault. She had a candle in a jam bottle, but the light went out, she said, just before she met the policeman.[29]

There were certainly many hazards – physical and legal – to be overcome on the roads leading to gaffs. Once arrived at their destination, the showmen were not always greeted with open arms. It was not just municipal authorities and residents' associations that were marshalling forces against them; Temperance Groups, viewing fairs as dens of iniquity, were also bringing pressure to bear.

At Chichester the Board of Guardians wanted to extend their Workhouse and deemed Sloe Fair field to be the best site for the new buildings. The Town Council immediately backed the guardians' campaign to abolish the fair on the pretext that it encouraged immorality and drunkenness. In 1904 the Salvation Army stationed itself near North Walls and men and women preachers warned people of the dangers of the fair. The event, however, attracted such dense crowds that it was almost impossible to walk around the field in the evening.

Gallopers and switchbacks were kept going from morn till night to the accompaniment of ear-piercing music. There were shooting galleries, coconut shies, gingerbread stalls, toy stalls, china emporia, penny trumpet merchants, Cheap Jacks, and fried fish vendors. Showmen invited people to walk up to see the first and last appearance of 'Bill Bailey', animated pictures, a calf with a dog's head. There was a deal of good-humoured play involving throwing of confetti and squirting of water.

The City Fathers were not pleased ... especially when townspeople suggested that the council could well learn a lesson or two from the showmen. For some time there had been agitation for street lighting in Chichester and the showmen had proved adept at harnessing electricity for the illumination of their roundabouts. In this respect 'these showmen are in advance of our town council,' complained the local newspaper.[30]

A year later it was remarked that 'The efforts made in some quarters to do away with that ancient and noisy festival, Sloe Fair, seem to have given it a new vitality ... Everybody, high and low, seemed to be gone to swell the crowd on those noisy acres, where the whirligigs whirled, and the steam sideshows hooted their various invitations.'[31]

Politics and popular pleasures often came together in surprising ways during these years. Harelip provided amusements for a Unionist Fête in Petworth Park organised by Lord Leconfield in July 1905. Among the illustrious speakers were Sir Edward Carson, Lord Talbot and Lord Turnour. They were gratified to see the Unionist cause could still muster some eight to nine thousand supporters in West Sussex, although it was a moot point as to whether the crowds came to listen to the speeches, enjoy the free tea, or ride on the roundabouts.[32]

Serious politics and showmen are not natural bedfellows. At Loxwood Show in 1906 the speeches were cut short by the proximity of a roundabout and coconut shy. Getting up to propose the Houses of Parliament, Mr Cattley began: "The House of Lords represents the mature thought of the nation;" ... (a burst of music from the roundabout urged *Won't you come back to Bombay?*) Mr Cattley wisely sat down. Lord Leconfield then stood to reply. "I do not," he said, "often go to the House of Lords; the debates are a little dull." ("Three shots a penny; now then, gentlemen, try your skill!" came a strident voice accompanied by *The Old Bull and Bush* from the organ.)[33]

"Politics is all very well," said Harelip, "for those as have leisure to enjoy 'em!"

No-one visiting Harting Fair in November 1907, when the village was so lively with Matthews's illuminated Merry-go-round in the Square,[34] could have realised how tenuous Harelip's link with that scene was becoming. There was a lot of money owing on his roundabout and he was falling further and further behind with the payments. Besides, Ria was no longer two hands on his back pushing him forward insistently towards success. Often she did nothing but complain that her man was not a bit of good to her, that she'd be better off getting a little place of her own to sell things from. She was talking about settling down. "But that'd mak' us no better'n flats," moaned Harelip. Even this failed to shake Ria. She had made up her mind.

Flash Ria had not mellowed with the years. "A tall, upstanding sort of woman with rather a regal personality" was how her daughter described her; "a right cow-bag", others said. She had borne ten

chavvies, eight of whom survived to adulthood. By the time the last came into the world in 1898 Ria had all but forgotten the anxiety with which she searched the face of each earlier infant. This time the dread caught her unawares when she saw that the child's features carried the stamp which had given rise to his father's nickname. Henry Lord Leonard, as he was christened, had harelip and cleft palate. There was nothing to be done for the condition in those days, so the little lad was left to develop his own very special brand of fortitude in life.

When her youngest son was ten years old Ria took a shop in Horsham, set up a secondhand clothing business and stayed put next Spring when Harelip took to the road. Not that this kept her free from conflict with the law, for its long arm reached out to touch her even in the sanctity of a house. In July 1909, as Harelip was being fined for allowing three horses to stray on London Road, Arundel, Ria was simultaneously being summonsed in Horsham for failing to send little Henry to school.[35]

Ria's business thrived, but the shop's profits availed her husband naught. Came the day when Savage's agents arrived from King's Lynn to re-possess the roundabout. Harelip could not bear to watch as the loads were secured and towed away. His friend, James Coneley, discovered him in a local bar. "They're taking it away, taking me roundabout away," Harelip sobbed, tears dripping into his beer.

Soon Ria moved down from Horsham to set up business in a shop she bought in Worthing. Her husband continued to travel with sidestuff during summer months and did logging in the winter. Pursuing his uneasy existence half on, half off the road, Harelip no longer had the heart to battle for pitches.

Henry Lord Leonard Matthews.

Chapter Ten

A SET OF GALLOPERS

I have seen it built up season after season from what was just an ordinary machine with plain rounding boards and brass rods to what must now be one of the finest and most beautiful rides in the country.
(*World's Fair*, 10 April 1937)

Heathfield in East Sussex is special for travellers and house-dwellers alike. According to tradition Spring is reborn each year when, at 'Hefful' Fair on 14 April, an old gypsy woman opens up her basket to let the first cuckoo fly free.

Harelip and Flash Ria had pulled into winter quarters with the Harrises near Heathfield just before the birth of their first child, and it was here on 11 January 1876 that Joe was born. Ria had examined the baby's face with more than usual trepidation before breathing out a deep sigh of relief.

Being eldest son in a showman's family meant growing up quickly; a chavvy became adult on the day he learned to give change. Joe went through this initiation when hardly more than six years old. He had little schooling, but from the moment he learned how to handle money he took responsibility for the family business, working alongside his father and the other menfolk, building up and pulling down, sharing their profits and joys, their worries and fears, fighting off their rivals, taking on their feuds.

Joe spent his youth travelling through Sussex and neighbouring counties with first his grandfather's and then his father's fair. No better apprenticeship existed for the preparation of a twentieth century showman. Notorious for his temper, he gradually learned to

draw on native wit rather than brute force to get what he wanted. Or, maybe it was that he had to survive as a showman in a world very different from that of his forefathers. The 'gavver-mush', no longer an amateurish fellow to be shoved aside, was now a trained law-enforcement officer backed by a municipal corporation and full panoply of justice set up by the house-dweller. Joe had to find a way of working with the new establishments in town and village.

He was lucky in his choice of a wife. Amy Rowland had been born in a wagon in Mill Lane, Guildford, in October 1874, to parents who were both from families that had travelled the South-East for generations.

Her mother, One-Eye Betsy, was sister to Andrew Smith. Her father, Tom Rowland, was nephew to Redshirt's wife, Polly, and thus one of the Bushnell (or Bushell) clan. In his youth he had been known as Tom Bushnell or Tom Smith until running foul of the law on a poaching charge. While awaiting trial he was lodged in Surrey's County Gaol, but soon managed to give warders the slip and escaped over the wall. Unfortunately, just as he got clear of the prison, a constable spotted him and gave chase. Tom made a dash for the river and swam across. 'The constable could not manage this and therefore was quite thrown off his scent.'[1]

The gavvers soon abandoned their search for a man called Smith, alias Bushell, leaving sixteen-year old Tom to set about establishing his lawful business under his mother's maiden name, Rowland.

He married Betsy before he was twenty and the 1881 Census records them as living in a meadow in Depot Road, Horsham, with their three children: Amy, Thomas and Billy. Tom's occupation is given as 'Hawker'. For the next few years they continued to travel to the same Sussex and Surrey fairs as their parents and grandparents had attended. Their annual circuit also took in Weyhill in Hampshire where on 14 October 1888 their son Joseph was christened and on 12 October 1890 their daughter Lavinia.

Joe Matthews.

Amy, née Rowland, wife of Joe Matthews.

Above: Amy and her little brothers.

Left: Tom Rowland's wagon – Amy's home before she married Joe Matthews.

Below: Three of Amy's brothers – Bill, Jack and Tom Rowland.

Tom Rowland's 'Pipe-heads' joint, known as the 'Wallops'.

However, in the 1890s while keeping their winter base at Station Road, Woking, Tom and Betsy began to explore further westward during late summer months, establishing a new circuit through Dorset, Wiltshire and Somerset. Their presence was welcomed in these places because Tom had painted up an attractive 'Pipe-heads' joint, popularly known as 'The Wallops', and his sons had grown adept at rattling up the attention of a crowd and keeping them amused.

At Glastonbury Tor Fair in September 1895 Betsy gave birth to Albert, her eighth surviving child. She had led a tempestuous life, being left blind in one eye in the course of a particularly violent family row at Thursley several years before. Now she was over forty and took a little while to recover from her confinement. Fortunately her two older daughters were able to take the strain from her.

Amy at twenty was a second mother to the new baby, while Priscilla, aged eleven, made herself useful in looking after the other chavvies. This was especially valuable in the weeks following Albert's birth when, one by one, the younger children went down with measles. However, by the time they pulled in to Mr Fowler's field near the West Mills for Bridport Fair in early October they had all recovered, except for Priscilla who was left with a racking cough. If she was no better, Betsy decided, they would call in a doctor at their next stopping-place, Sherborne.

Sherborne Pack Monday Fair followed immediately on from Bridport and by now had become a regular fixture on the Rowlands' calendar. It was held on the first Monday after Old Michaelmas Day, 10 October. Although tradition associated it with the day in 1490 when masons 'packed up' their tools on the completion of their work on the restored abbey-church, more likely its name was connected with the 'pacts', or labour engagements, entered into between farmer and newly-hired servants at what was the start of a new agricultural year.

Whatever its origins, Pack Monday Fair was a great annual occasion in Sherborne, full of life, colour, and noise – heralded over-night by 'rough music' and the parading of the streets by 'Teddy Roe's Band' blowing horns and bugles, bashing tin-trays, pots and pans and drums.

Dorset County Chronicle described the event in 1895:

SHERBORNE PACK MONDAY FAIR was held on Monday in lovely autumnal weather and during the day the streets were thronged. The Pleasure Fair was particularly well supplied this year, but the effect of the great gathering of travellers was marred by a division – one part, the major portion, pitching their property in Half Moon field, whilst the others found a temporary home in the Antelope field. The diocesan missioner, the Rev.J.Swinstead, held a service in the Half Moon field on Sunday afternoon but the majority of the showmen had not then arrived from Bridport. He gave an eloquent address in the Abbey in the morning and in the evening preached at the St Paul's Mission Church.

At Midnight the renowned Teddy Roe's Band perambulated the town as of yore, but the hideous row was of much milder form than usual, although some 200 persons took part, being accompanied by many females.

The attractions in the Half Moon field were most numerous, and whilst Brewer's steam roundabouts came in for a lot of patronage, there were the Grand Spanish Menagerie, containing an untameable African lion and a sea-lion, the monster woman and the tiniest man in the world, and a boxing saloon with female boxers as well as male. Highflyers, coconut bowling, shooting ranges, and many other amusements were to be found here, and attracted the chief portion of the pleasure seekers.

In the Antelope field Heal's steam roundabouts, which at night were lighted by electricity, Townsend's miniature roundabouts, highflyers, and shooting galleries were erected.

On the Parade and around St John's buildings were stalls with sweets and gingerbread nuts, toys, fancy articles. And though the streets were so crowded not a single case came before the magistrates the next morning and the police are to be commended for their vigilant and patient conduct.[2]

And so for most people the Pack fair had passed off agreeably. However, for Tom and Betsy the event was altogether over-shadowed by the worsening condition of Priscilla. They had called in Dr Atkinson as soon as they arrived in *Half Moon* field. By a sad coincidence he had just come from the deathbed of the daughter of the cemetery-keeper who, almost exactly Priscilla's age, had suddenly died from the effects of eating yew berries. Dr Atkinson immediately called on the services of the town nurse to help Betsy tend her sick child, but to no avail. On Thursday morning Priscilla died from inflammation of the lungs, an aftermath of measles.

The funeral took place on the following Monday with crowds watching silently while four lads carried the prettily carved coffin to the cemetery and all the travellers followed carrying flowers.[3]

People of Sherborne remembered the family's tragedy and went out of their way to welcome the Rowlands when they returned for Pack Monday Fair the following year. The Diocesan Missioner, the Reverend Jacob, calling to ask how they were, was delighted to find Betsy lying-in after the birth of another child – a girl barely one week old. Then and there, in the wagon, he christened her Janie.[4]

Soon after this Tom and Betsy took to wintering in Market Yard, Frome, and it was here that Joseph Matthews arrived on 10 February 1899 to marry their eldest daughter.

Amy was small, with long sandy gold hair wrapped round her head in twisted coils. She had a freckled elfin face, ageless grey eyes and sweet smile that belied a reputation for a tongue as tart as a berry. Her sleeves were typically rolled up above elbows to free her arms for work. She liked to wear pretty patterned blouses and a dark skirt protected by layers of commodious pinafores. When she was minding the stuff, or if company came, she peeled off one or more pinafores. No matter whom she was with, their status in her estimation could be gauged by the number of pinafores she had discarded on their behalf. She was fastidious in manner and dress, not talking a great deal, softly smiling as if enjoying a private joke with life.

Amy, her wagon and children.

Amy with her youngest daughter, Beatie.

Amy Matthews in front of her living-wagon.

Although Joe already had his own hoopla and darts stall, he and Amy continued to travel with Harelip so that he could lend his father a hand with the building-up of the roundabout and heavier stuff. For Amy, used to family strife, life appeared to be one long battle as the feud between the Matthewses and her uncle, Andrew Smith, continued unabated.

The first winter after their marriage Joe pulled their wagon into a field behind the Norfolk Arms Hotel, Worthing. In the following January, Amy bore a son, christened in honour of his father and his birthplace – Joseph Norfolk. Then, at the end of

Louie and her twin sisters, Annie and Amy.

October 1902, while pulled in at Arundel behind another public house, Amy gave birth to a daughter. Though christened Jubilee Louisa Maria, she was never called by any name other than Louie. The new baby had a harelip but, mercifully, no cleft palate.

"It's a shame it's touched a rakli," Amy said. "Still, now the hare's had his three, he won't be back for more."

She proved right. Thomas Henry Matthews was born with face unblemished on 27 November 1906 and christened at Headley on 13 January 1907. Later that year Joe joined forces with his cousin's husband, Dicky Wall, who had engaged to provide amusements at Beach House Park, Worthing, over Easter. The main attraction was Wall's steam roundabout, popular with all except those living in nearby Madeira Avenue who complained vigorously about the noise. An action was brought and Joe was called upon to give evidence in court that everything possible had been done to minimise the sound. The case went against them and Wall was fined £3.10s.6d.[5]

In former days the incident would have passed unnoticed by the wider travelling fraternity. After 1904 showmen could read all about such happenings in their own newspaper, the *World's Fair*, and this journal became both instrument and reflection of changing attitudes in the profession. Travelling showmen realised that their survival depended on presenting themselves as a responsible section of society. Their leaders took matters in hand.

In 1910 U.K.S.V.D.A. changed its name to the Showmen's Guild and began more actively to regulate life on the tobers as well as continuing to promote the good image of the fairground. 'Easter Hints' published in the columns of the *World's Fair* illustrates how showmen constantly urged each other on to improve their public relations.[6]

See that you have all your water tanks full up. Nothing worse than a water dandy being pushed through a crowded fairground.

See to the lights before darkness comes on – be ready.

Get extra 'munjari' in the wagon for Easter. Remember many of the shops will be closed for the holiday.

The banks will also be closed for Easter Monday. I hope you will go on Tuesday 'with the load'

Don't forget to be smart and tidy, all of you, even when closed down on the Sunday.

Don't disturb the neighbourhood that day by knocking and shouting and singing. Perhaps these people won't like it, and, after all, it is THEIR territory, NOT YOURS.

On the whole showman prospered during the pre-war years, but they did not remain unaffected by dangerous rifts in society. The Hancock family in Devon was made painfully aware of the struggle to obtain Votes for Women. In December, 1913, two postcards from Devonport were delivered simultaneously to 'J. Matthews, Show Vans, Star Field, Havant, Hants.'

Amy, who could not read or write, listened as Joe read the carefully penned messages from her brother, Albert Rowland:

Dear Joe and Amy,
I am sending postcards of Hancocks Fire. It has completely ruined there machines and organ but we saved roundabouts and trucks with a tussle you can see it was a tidy fire through timber. The fire was caused through sufragettes catching fire to Timber yard it as nearly ruined them. We are all well Hoping you are the same.

Albert

Their ground is just away from ours.

Above: Postcard from Devonport showing Hancock's fire.

Below: Two postcards with first-hand account of Hancock's fire.

The Hancocks were an old-established West Country firm run by two brothers and their sister. Despite valiant attempts to combat the blaze, their losses were enormous. Under the orders of Miss Sophie Hancock everyone worked his hardest, and none more so than the lady herself, as was shown by her hands which were badly burned and had to be attended to by ambulancemen. Their switchback railway was destroyed and their gallopers, though saved, were blistered by the intense heat. Damage was estimated at £2000 and the family never recovered from the disaster.[7]

Tom and Betsy Rowland had meanwhile continued their migration westward, spending their winter months at Richmond Walk in Devonport. Their

Tom Rowland's chair-o-planes with its Gaudin organ.

Bill Rowland next to Tasker tractor *Princess Mary*.

Jack's daughter Ruby Pannell, later Rowland.

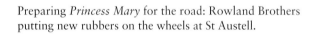

Amy's brother-in-law, Jack Pannell, at Helston Plum fair.

Preparing *Princess Mary* for the road: Rowland Brothers putting new rubbers on the wheels at St Austell.

annual circuit now took in Corpus Christi Fair at Penzance.

Up to about 1884 Penzance had enjoyed two pleasure fairs: Corpus Christi and Midsummer Quay Fair. The former, which took place on the first Thursday after Trinity Sunday and lasted three days, was held in the narrow Alverton Lane, causing traffic obstruction between Penzance and St Just. This problem was overcome when it transferred to the Recreation Ground.

However, after the turn of the century, friction was generated by the levying of tolls by the Corporation and early skirmishes eventually erupted into what has gone down in the annals of Penzance as 'The Battle of Corpus Christi.'

In 1906 the Corporation levied a toll of £10 on each roundabout and a similar amount for shows. The show proprietors objected and suggested that the ground should be let by tender. So, the following year this course was adopted and the tenders ranged from £15 to £20 per roundabout or show. The Corporation were smiling. Then in 1908 some half-a-dozen showmen combined forces to treat for better terms and offered two shillings per diameter foot of space occupied. The Corporation maintained that the letter was so dictatorial in tone as almost to place it out of court. The dispute dragged on until all remained to be decided in the field on Monday, 15 June.

The Cornishman, 18 June 1908, takes up the story:

THE BATTLE OF CORPUS CHRISTI
Arrival of the Invaders
Frontal attack and turning movements.

The invasion by the combined forces of circular cavalry, armoured switchback railway, aerial swing boats, scouts, brass bands, and other mounted infantry forces assumed a serious aspect on Monday night.

The combined forces were utterly routed on their first attempt on the Recreation Ground, and it was decided not to assail that position again.

General Hancock, Captain Rowland, Brigadier Brewer, and Miss Hancock as the modern Joan of Arc held a council of war. After sending scouts throughout the neighbourhood, they endeavoured to find a weak point in the fortifications. They almost effected an entrance both to the east and west of the town, but the Council Brigade acting in concert with the Land Owners' League, concentrated their fire and the attacking forces were again repulsed.

Excitement in the borough ran high, and the utmost consternation prevailed. The juveniles hoped that the invaders would either camp on the Promenade or storm the Recreation Ground, and

gain entrance on their own terms. The tradespeople wondered if their goods would be commandeered and if so whether the Corporation would pay the bill. The Council Brigade wondered what would happen when the war budget had to be faced, and the burghers would find themselves saddled with an extra rate of a half-penny in the £. All was suspense and when a charge was fixed at Penlee Quarry some inexperienced visitors wondered if the artillery had opened fire. In the meantime General Hancock and staff officers were seen in an armoured locomotive speeding about the district. Whether their object was to capture the Mayor and hold him as hostage, or whether they were bent on abducting the Market Committee, was not apparent.

The situation was so serious that we have engaged war correspondents to go to the sea front or any other point from which operations can be watched.

HEAMOOR, Monday Night.
Our Heamoor correspondent writes:

Messrs Hancock, Brewer, Anderton and Rowland, yesterday arranged with Mr J.K White, Boscathnoe to take the field known as 'Poltair Lawn' and which is situated at the foot of Madron hill. The above showmen have taken the whole of this spacious field, and will sub-let to the smaller show people. The event has caused quite a sensation in the place. In all probability the fair will be in full swing on Wednesday night.

CAUSEWAYHEAD, 1.45 p.m.
Irate Townsman:

I suppose this is what those – Methodys have done. They've built a chapel up there and are now keeping the Show Brigade out.

PARADE STREET, 2 p.m.
Ratepayer:

I'm with the Corporation. Let the Council save their dignity even if we lose the money. Why should we take it lying down? If we lose the £140 we can still live on bread splits and gingerbread nuts. I shall go to Poltair, but not often, and in the dark when they won't know I'm a Penzance man.

MARKET JEW STREET, 2.5 p.m.
Captain Rowland's staff:

Yes, we hear that one of our big machine guns with a platoon of cavalry has gained entrance to Poltair. The Colonel has withdrawn his opposition and has ratified the treaty with Field Marshall White.

Then the armoured train with baggage moved on in the direction of Heamoor.

MORRAB GARDENS, 2.15 p.m.
BURGESS:

I say it is a thundering shame. Why should we lose £140 and tramp a mile? It will cost £10 to put the ground in order again, but the Council could have made a clear gain of £100.

FAIR PLAY asks:

Why is it that we are to have no fair at Penzance this year, and what right have a few men (who are supposed to represent the ratepayers) to prevent its continuance by imposing impossible tolls? Some of us are unable to do anything in the matter at present, but perhaps we may have something to say next November.

They did, and the combined voices of the ratepayers and showmen delivered Corpus Christi safely back into the Recreation Ground where Tom and Betsy were pictured a few years later in front of their stall. Tom had by now grown so stout that he had to carve their dining-table into a crescent to enable him to sit near his food.

Meanwhile in the South-East many old established fairs were also being threatened by municipal tidying up operations. In 1910 Hambledon District Council appealed to the Home Secretary for an Order abolishing Haslemere Charter Fair which had been in existence since Tudor times. Formerly the tolls of what was primarily a cattle fair had been devoted to the upkeep of an almshouse. The tolls were abandoned by the early nineteenth century, and no cattle were brought in for sale after 1903. The pleasure fair had been moved in 1905 to land owned by the Council at Clay Hill. Now it was alleged that whenever pressure was brought to bear on the showmen they threatened to move back to their traditional pitches in the High Street, so the Order of Abolition was sought as means to gain effective police control for the future.[8]

Old annual cattle and sheep fairs were fast fading away as farmers preferred to send their stock to periodic town markets. In 1912 it was noted that there was entire absence of cattle for sale at Farnham Midsummer fair[9] and Crawley September fair,[10] and at Sloe fair, once famous for its horses, only one was actually on offer.[11] The following year flock-masters who had annually journeyed to St John's Fair, Burgess Hill, and to Lindfield Fair informed the clerks of these ancient institutions that they would no longer be attending in view of the declining number of lambs being penned.[12]

Nevertheless, what concerned most people in Lindfield and the surrounding area was the fate of their pleasure fair which they pleaded to be allowed to keep. The authorities, aware how important the Fair receipts were in their financial strategy, listened sympathetically. The Parish Council's recent attempts to raise money by swan-culture had not been successful – six cygnets at half-a-sovereign each when

Amy's mother, One-eye Betsy, and father, Tom Rowland.

set against an annual corn bill for the keep of parent swans left little margin for reducing the rates! The Pleasure Fair with its receipts of about £60 and expenses of £10 was far more profitable, and so it was allowed to remain on the Common.[13]

Mitcham Fair during recent years had provided something of a test case. From time immemorial this three-day affair had been held from 12 August on the Green. In 1907 the Smiths and Matthews family joined with about six hundred showmen from all parts of the country who descended on the Green to erect their booths, rides and shows in combined resistance to moves by the Conservators of Mitcham Common to abolish the fair.

Events were watched carefully by a special force of police, and representatives of the Conservators as well as of the Showmen's Guild. In the evening a public meeting, convened in the centre of the fairground, was addressed by the Reverend T. Horne, chaplain of the Guild, and several members of Mitcham Parish Council before resolutions were passed protesting against the Conservators' actions in trying to prohibit this ancient fair. The showmen expressed their willingness that it should be moved to another part of the Common.

The following day the fair opened without any opposition from the Conservators, although the showmen were warned that legal proceedings would be taken against them individually.[14] The High Court battles which ensued ended in stalemate and Mitcham Fair was preserved for posterity. Many showmen were there in 1914 soon after outbreak of war. General uncertainty and reduced coverage in the daily press meant fewer visitors. Then came a dramatic descent by War Office representatives who made a raid on the horses, taking away twenty-six. Bankers' drafts given in payment were scant compensation for loss of faithful animals which had pulled their wagons hundreds of miles from fair to fair.[15] After the horses, the traction engines were requisitioned for military work. As a consequence larger loads could not be transported, and one of the last gaffs of the season, Petworth Fair on 22 November, fell completely flat.[16] Once war had been declared the Showmen's Guild made known that showmen, like every other decent section of the community, were sending their sturdiest sons into the army. Week by week the World's Fair published proud photographs of Showland's latest recruits, followed all too often by sad little notices of their deaths in service of King and Country. Showmen sent more than three thousand sons to the Front as well as providing several ambulances paid for by the Guild.

For Joe the early days of war brought desperate anxiety as he wondered how in the circumstances he was to earn a living for his family. Amy had just given birth to another child so there were now four boys and five girls. In order of age they were Joseph, Louie, Betsy Rose, Thomas, William, John, Amy and Annie (twins), and the baby, Beatrice. The answer to Joe's dilemma came in the form of a contract to drive his own traction engine when it was commandeered for government service. This change in their fortunes compelled the family to seek settled quarters for the

Amy (2nd left) and her nine children in front of one of their first traction engines.

The twins at school in Liphook c.1918 – Annie centre of 3rd row, Amy 3rd from left of back row.

Joseph Norfolk Matthews, one of Showland's recruits for the First World War.

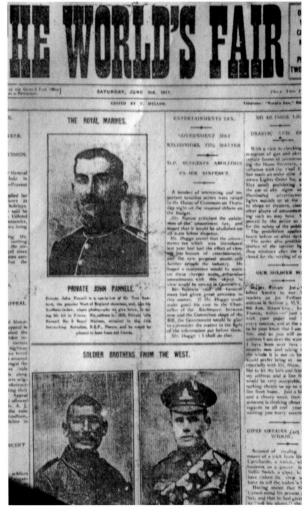

World's Fair reports Joe and Albert Rowland and Jack Pannell going off to War.

Henry, Prissy, and Bill Castle. Their mother was Rachel, sister of One-eye Betsy.

FOR Sale,
cheap, "The Kaiser" cost £15 last summer (Lawrence's make), with new 10ft. frame and new tilting, cost £6 10s. for same; and ball and ball bins. A good money taker. The cause of selling, owner gone to the front. For price and full particulars apply to—
Mr. W. Morris,
83, Timbercroft Lane,
Plumstead Common, Kent.

Advert from *World's Fair*, 4 December 1915.

Emily Beatrice Colbourne, née Matthews, who died in the 'flu epidemic, 1918.

The grave of Emily and Moses at Broadwater Green.

Matthews's family among group on Janie Cole's Switchback c.1919.

first time in their lives, and the home they found was a railway carriage in Liphook where they stayed for the duration of the war.

Mitcham Fair continued to be held annually – though but a dim shadow of its former self after fear of zeppelins caused police to ban naphtha flares and large electric lamps.[17] In 1916 showmen at the event gave one day's proceeds to the Guild's ambulance fund; their donations reflecting the benefit from an extra hour's daylight recently introduced.[18] Nevertheless, what with military service, their women going into munitions work and loss of traction engines, far fewer travellers attended Mitcham Fair

Group including Matthewses and Coles, 1919.

in 1918. Those who did earned the gratitude of the 'boys in blue', glad to find something to brighten the monotony of an invalid's life.[19]

November 1918 saw peace being celebrated throughout the land. In contrast, the Matthews family gathered together sadly for the funerals of Joe's younger brother and sister. Moses, as a member of the Army Service Corps, had been sent to a training camp at Bury St Edmunds, but was soon invalided back to his family suffering from tuberculosis. He was nursed by Ria and his sister Beatrice. When he died, Beatrice fell victim to the influenza epidemic and survived him by only a few days. They were buried in the same grave at Broadwater Green.

In 1919 Joe returned to travelling the fairs with an assortment of sideshows – hoopla, darts, coconut shy and touch-'ems – all games of skill, he maintained. PC Andrews disagreed. At Slocumb fairground, near Gosport, he threw fifteen rings at Joe's hoopla stall with little success. His colleague, PC Vimy, stood for ten minutes counting 165 hoops being thrown and not one managed to secure a half-crown prize. The matter was brought to court. Joe was charged with contravening the Betting Act of 1853 by running hoopla, a game of chance, not skill. Joe's solicitor antagonised the policemen. He implied that their case rested on the fact that they personally lacked the degree of skill needed to play hoopla successfully.

"I'll wager you couldn't ring one of the half-crowns in a hundred throws," said PC Vimy. The

Ada, Louie and Rosie with Little Johnny Matthews in the background.

Ada and Clara being driven by Rosie.

solicitor, not being a gambling man, declined the challenge. Joe was fined two pounds.[20]

After this Joe purchased larger hoops and made stands suitable to hold bulkier prizes such as groceries. He pinned up a painted placard stating: 'The Prizes on this stall are manufactured by J. Lyons & Co. Ltd., Cadby Hall, London. This guarantees their quality and value.' At Littlehampton Fair, 1923, an Urban Councillor was seen smugly carrying off a jar of jam he had just won.[21]

The Mulo-mush continued to make his presence felt by rapping at wagon doors. Joe's father, Harelip, died in 1921, followed quite soon by Uncle Redshirt in 1922, and Amy's mother, One-eye Betsy, in 1923. As for the next generation, Joe's children were growing up, sturdy and intelligent; he wanted the best for them. Whenever they stayed more than a few days in the same place, the younger ones were sent to school and they all learned to read and write.

But what was there to hold them together, give

John Matthews left on big wheel of Tasker tractor. Cousins: Beatie, Ada and Rosie and Johnny Matthews (little boy). John's brother Tom, 2nd from Right.

Ada – with Gaudin organ from Joe's gallopers on left.

Centre engine of Joe's gallopers.

Joe Coneley and the girls. The caged birds were to attract the public.

Joe, Amy and other showmen visit the World's Fair, Agricultural Hall, Islington.

Right: Joe, Amy, Bill (Joe's brother) and Naomi (brother John's wife) in Darts' stall.

Joe and Amy minding their Darts' stall.

The five daughters of Joe and Amy.

Right: Louie minding the Darts' stall while Prince Galitzin tests his skill.

Portrait of Louie and Rosie, taken at Southampton.

'The Little Girls' – Amy, Annie and Beatie.

'The Little Girls' grow up – Beatie, Amy and Annie, 1935.

sense of purpose, represent to the family something more than mere survival in a harsh world? In his mid-forties Joe conceived an ambition to succeed where his own father had failed. He would become a Riding Master.

In fairground terms a 'Riding Master' was a man who, like Uncle Redshirt, owned one or more machines, was able to negotiate as lessee at important fairs and then organise and sub-let the ground to other lesser showmen. After all, a fair was hardly a fair without some modern riding-machine, but these represented large sums of capital investment. For years now Joe and Amy had been saving.

Casting around for an opportunity, Joe saw an advertisement for a secondhand set of gallopers offered for sale by Bates, a Lancashire firm of showmen. Taking his two eldest sons, he set off to inspect it and immediately clinched the deal. The roundabout was brought back to Star Meadow, Havant, where under the gaze of the rest of the family Joe and the Boys set to building it up for the first time. Amy watched the dilapidated horses and broken wooden platform pieces being unpacked. She said nothing, but lifted the corner of her pinafore to wipe away tears of disappointment.

Their own set of gallopers – the idea had appealed to Amy as much as it had to Joe. She had pictured to herself the wonderful roundabout that her cousin, Tom Smith, had purchased from Redshirt. They were always meeting up with it on their travels; no other ride could stand against it.

Commissioned from Savages of King's Lynn by Daniel Cooper in 1897, the top of its centre truck had been decorated with canvas portraits of the Cooper family. These were still on the machine when it was sold to Tom Smith. He also inherited the chap who looked after the roundabout, and who had passed with it from Dan Cooper to Redshirt Matthews and on to Tom Smith, like a serf of old, except that in his case Horace King bound himself not to the soil, but to the machine he loved. More than once he risked life and eventually lost limb in its service.

Wearing his usual moleskin trousers, he was on top of the centre truck oiling the cranks when someone started up the ride. The sound of the organ drowned out his shouts and no one knew anything was wrong until they saw blood dripping down. By the time the machine came to a halt, Horace's leg was so badly mangled it had to be amputated. He lost two fingers as well. Even these terrible injuries did not lessen his passion for the roundabout that he swore never to leave. Nevertheless, there were times when it was hard to keep that vow.

There came a day when Horace, or Peg (Peg-leg)

Tom Smith's gallopers being built up.

Tom Smith's gallopers almost built up.

Horace 'Peg' King, one of Tom's loyal Chaps.

as he was now called, was involved in a bitter row with his employer. Angry words were exchanged. Peg threatened to leave. Tempers flared.

"I'll be damned if you will," said Tom, fetching an axe. The blade fell with deadly force – again and again. Within seconds Peg's wooden leg had been chopped into small pieces. When the heat of the moment was past, Tom did his best to make amends. He found to hand the very thing needed to improvise a new limb. With a bit of ingenuity he modified a coconut stand which for some time stood Peg in good stead, and he certainly stayed on with the roundabout.

Tom Smith's set of gallopers took pride of place at Littlehampton's annual fair on 25 May 1924 with its bright striped tilt, ornate carved heads of kings picked out in gold leaf on the rounding boards, gleaming brass spiralled rods, and magnificently painted beasts. It was built up on the beach at Fisherman's Hard, right up against the high water mark. Originally the roundabout had consisted of ostriches only, but at the time he purchased it Tom exchanged eighteen ostriches for eighteen horses from another roundabout in Redshirt's possession so that thereafter each ride travelled with both horses and birds as mounts.

Advert
For Sale – one set of Gallopers with 36 birds, with Gavioli Organ (28 keys), four trucks in all, good working order. To be seen at work at Mr Mayne's ground, no.7, Curtain Road, Shoreditch, all the Christmas. Also fitted with Hayne's electric light and dynamo.

Wanted to Sell, set of gallopers with 24 horses, 12 cockerells, Barrel Organ (makers, Chiappa & Sons), Electric light, Dynamo, four trucks; all in good working order, to be sold cheap. Apply Wm Matthews, Gravel Road, Farnborough.
(World's Fair, 7 December 1912)

Tom Smith's gallopers – platform being fitted.

Tom Smith's gallopers built up.

Tom Smith's gallopers ready to leave Victoria Park, Haywards Heath, in1938.

Mrs Tom Smith on her wagon steps.

Tom Smith's gallopers at Littlehampton Fair, 1924 (Andrew Smith in foreground).

Littlehampton Fair, 26 May 1924.

Right: Marina derelict at the Smiths' yard in Shoreham.

Below: Surrey Street, Littlehampton – arrival of the fair, 25 May 1925.

Littlehampton Fair, 26 May 1925.

Amy had expected the roundabout that Joe brought back from Lancashire to be of similar quality to Tom Smith's. Instead, it appeared plain and tawdry, its rotted woodwork having suffered further damage in transit. However, the deal was done and they would have to get on and make the best of it. Amazingly, even on that very first evening at Havant, the gallopers attracted unexpectedly enthusiastic response from the public. It took money for them and it continued to take money. Encouraged, Joe and his sons put their energy into refurbishing the machine.

It was a three-abreast ride manufactured by Savage in 1893 and fitted with an 87 Key Marenghi organ. In April 1924 it opened for a few weeks at the

The Marenghi organ – later replaced by a Gaudin.

Norfolk Quay Pavilion and Grounds, Littlehampton, but could not rival Tom Smith's gallopers when both families provided amusements at the annual Littlehampton Fair on 25 May.[22] The trouble was, there was not always room for new rides at the traditional fair sites. Indeed, many showmen who arrived in Littlehampton on 24 May were unable to find positions and had to go away without opening. Trade was also being hit by the general depression in the country. Unemployment and the high cost of living did not leave much money in people's pockets to spend on pleasure. It became clear to Joe that he would have to work hard to build up a run of sites to accommodate the new roundabout, but in the early days he was limited by the means of transport at his disposal.

To start with, he owned only two small Tasker tractors which were quite adequate as long as he worked 'on the Level', the Southampton-Brighton coastal run, but would not suffice to draw heavy loads over the South Downs. The light steam tractors had proved popular with showmen because, from 1903 to the Heavy Motor Cars Act of 1923, traction engines of under five tons were permitted to travel at speeds of up to five miles per hour – an advantage over the heavier vehicles that were still limited to two m.p.h. through villages and towns, and four on the

Beatie, Amy and Cousin Rosie on Joe's Model T Ford, known as 'Tin Lizzie'.

Beatie in 'Tin Lizzie'.

Joe Matthews on left. His young brother, Henry Lord Leonard, front passenger in 'Tin Lizzie'.

Right: Charley Stroud driving a four-seater bull nose Morris with his sisters, May and Lil, in the back and Will Beldom (Lil's husband) in front.

Jerry Russett and group including some Matthews chavvies waiting to 'pull on' to Southampton Common.

open road. The light-weight traction engines also required only one person to handle them; even Joe's daughters were adept at driving the 'Little Giants'.

Before the war Joe had bought one tractor of this class, Tasker 1342, a three-ton compound engine which had been built in 1905. The family named it *Mighty Atom* and it bore the licence number AA 2025. After the war he bought a heavier version, Tasker 1595, a five-tonner built in 1914 and bearing the licence number AA 5264. This one was christened *Pride of Sussex*.

The family grew very fond of these engines, treating them with more respect than is usually accorded to machines even by owners whose livelihood depends on their smooth running. The engines and equipment embodied the family's pride in themselves and their reputation: *J. MATTHEWS & SONS* emblazoned along the canopies, the disc flywheels decorated in gold scrollwork, spiral brass rods highly polished. Like their heavier counterparts, these doughty machines were multi-purpose – they had a dynamo for generating electricity and their back axles were fitted with a winding winch carrying about fifty yards of wire rope. Joe and the Boys found this

Tasker 1595 *Pride of Sussex*.

Pride of Sussex.

90

Louie driving *Mighty Atom*, one of the Tasker Little Giants, at Portslade.

Mighty Atom, a 3-ton Tasker, at Portslade.

Tasker with little Johnny, son of John and Naomi Matthews.

Pulborough floods, 1924.

equipment a godsend when wiring the loads out of Pulborough floods in the summer of 1924.

Joe's sons were all highly skilled mechanics. They repaired, refurbished and decorated the family's equipment themselves. The high quality of the paintwork often excited people's interest.

"Who do you find to decorate the rides and engines so beautifully?" they were always asking.

"Ah, that was done by our Tom" was the usual reply.

To start with, Tom, assisted by his sister Annie, turned his attention to painting panels on the centre truck and on the rounding boards. Jungle beasts; wild birds, scarlet-plumed; tropical lush undergrowth: Tom was enjoying himself. As he grew in confidence, his painting exploded colour and life. By 1926 Matthews' Grand Electric Steeplechasers were attracting attention along the south coast. Electric? Lit up by electricity, the roundabout was, of course, still steam-driven. Joe simply made use of the term because anything 'electric' suggested modernity and excitement.

Shoreham Carnival, 1 September 1926: dancing in front of the Town Hall; confetti battles; a great sports programme culminating in a regatta with illuminated boats and fireworks. All the town en fête, thronging the amusements supplied for the occasion by J.Matthews & Sons. Chief source of delight – Joe's roundabout.[23]

Instead of pulling in to winter quarters after the backend fairs that winter, Joe rented Bainton's Yard, near the top end of Lake Road, Portsmouth, from 11 December over the Christmas period. He intended to run a small fair there, and applied for a music licence for an organ to attract children. He assured the magistrates that the noise would not be enough to annoy residents, but the Bench refused his application.[24]

During the next few months Tom got busy with his paint-brush again. By Portslade Easter Fair in 1928 the roundabout had been completely redecorated and was described as 'undoubtedly one of the prettiest sets of gallopers on the South Coast'. Each evening during the fair the machine provided a sight of dazzling splendour. Large crowds gathered round, listening to the latest songs and selections played by its new organ.[25]

Joe had replaced the smaller instrument with an 89 Key Gaudin organ bought from Horam and Lakin. The extra two keys played violin baritone but, being bigger, the new organ had to be cut down on either side to fit into the centre of the gallopers. Even then the platform only just missed it as it turned round. The Gaudin was a great improvement and loved for its particularly sweet-toned sound. Joe made a practice of inviting children to enjoy a free ride when the gallopers opened up each afternoon. *Sussex by the Sea*, his favourite tune, was always the first book of music played. At the end of the day other showmen recognised their signal to close down when they heard the Gaudin piping out its owner's signature: *Poor Joe*.

After the ground was cleared of strangers, with generators turned off and tilts laced up, the family gathered round the fire-drum to drink cocoa. They worked well together, Joe's sons and daughters; he was proud of them. His sense of well-being, their happiness, were woven into the fabric of the gallopers and during these years transformed into something golden.

Gallopers being built up in Star Meadow, Havant.

Something 'Golden'.

Chapter Eleven
ROAD MONARCHS

They have the smartest tackle touring Sussex, with an excellent reputation for keeping it so,
but not without hard work on the part of the members of Mr Matthews' family.

(*World's Fair*, 22 September 1934)

Visitors to Shoreham in 1928 thrilled to the sight of a powerful road locomotive, its rich ruby paintwork lined out in gold, sparkling spiralled brass rods supporting a canopy which read: *J. MATTHEWS & SONS WORLD'S FAIR.* Joe had purchased the ten horse power Fowler 13047, licence number DP 3863. Manufactured in 1914 and sold new to the War Department, it had seen active service in France during World War I, survived being bogged down in the Flanders mud to return to Britain where it was bought by Charles Openshaw of Reading. Openshaw converted the engine to showmen's type and sold it to Joe, who named it *Wanderer*.

Fowler road locomotive, *Wanderer.*

Wanderer was joined in Joe's stable by a companion, the six horse power Burrell 3542, licence number ND 472, the following year. It was given the name *Sunny South*. Although, as far as manufacturers were concerned, by 1930 the day of the traction engine was over, for showmen these monarchs of the road were still the acme of desire.

As with the Taskers, *Wanderer* and *Sunny South* were multi-purpose, able to haul loaded trucks and wagons from fair to fair and serving as a mobile

Amy and some of the family in front of Burrell engine *Sunny South.*

Joe's nephews, Ben Colbourne and Bernard Hall, standing next to the mighty wheel of the *Wanderer.*

Wanderer – Henry Lord Leonard standing on right.

Sunny South parked by the roadside at Horsham in July, 1932.

Wanderer and Joe's set of gallopers (before spiral rods and new domes and drops had been fitted).

power station whilst the fair was open. A belt-driven dynamo mounted on a steel platform in front of their chimneys generated electric current for the lights. Both engines possessed full length canopied roofs on top of which rested long chimney extensions ready to be affixed if the fair was held in streets or market squares where it was necessary to carry the smoke well away above nearby windows and doors.

In course of time three of Joe's sons became identified with the job of driving the big engines. Johnny drove *Wanderer*, Bill *Sunny South*, and Tom *Pride of Sussex*. Buying Welsh steam hard from local coal merchants was no problem, but picking up water was sometimes difficult. Each engine carried about three hundred gallons of water in its tanks as well as an emergency supply in the two-wheeled dandy,

hitched behind the last truck. They normally managed to journey fifteen miles before needing to stop at a watering-place. In the middle of a dry summer, however, some villagers would try to prevent showmen from sucking more water from their depleted ponds.

Wanderer – Bill Matthews
on left next to Harry
Stroud. Ben Coneley
crouching.

Centre-truck of the gallopers. Joe's brother John on right.

One of Joe's main reasons for buying the Fowler and Burrell was to increase his power when transporting loads across the South Downs. Bury Hill and Steep, near Petersfield, were notoriously difficult to negotiate.

"Push up!" Amy would shout to her daughters when they were going up hill. More urgently would come her shout when they started downhill: "Hold! Hold back!" The girls were then expected to grab the backs of the loads. When they were moving down particularly steep hills the girls took long poles from the packing truck ready to thrust through the wheels

Sunny South at Old Deer Park, Richmond, after purchase by John Beach.

and lodge them in the leaf springs. Many a pole snapped under the strain, but such primitive braking measures, in addition to drag shoes, prevented the wagons rolling down too quickly.

Taking loads downhill when water in the tank was getting low meant the engine-driver risked 'dropping the plug' – a term used when the fusible lead plug in the fire-box crown plate melted as a safety precaution against the boiler exploding. A 'dropped plug' was a real nuisance. The steam and water released put the fire out, and the driver had to wait for the engine to cool down before he could attempt to deal with the problem. This happened on one occasion to a showman travelling with Joe's fair. When his sister

Wanderer at Bognor, 1950, out of use.

Wanderer at Rudgwick, July 1940.

came up to the engine driver and asked what was wrong, he cursed and said he had dropped the plug, that's what was wrong. The girl had not heard the expression before. She walked back up the road bent double trying to find the 'dropped plug'.

The 1929 season opened with J. Matthews & Sons' amusements at Portslade-on-Sea for the beginning of April before moving on for the Easter holiday at Worthing where there were two fairs. Tom Smith and Sons opened at Brougham Road while Joe took ground at West Tarring. Further west along the coast that weekend Dicky Wall opened at Chichester and Janie Cole's scenic railway was at Emsworth.[1] Meanwhile, Joe had pulled off a coup. He secured concessions for Brighton Racehill Fairs and in 1929 advertised spaces to let for all kinds of fairground attractions at the Spring, August, and October meetings.[2] The Spring Races were held on 26-29 June with all the ground being measured out at eleven o'clock on 25 June. Bright three-coloured posters distributed for miles around guaranteed success for

the event.[3] Joe had cause for self-congratulation when the stuff was pulled down at the close of the race meeting and the loads took to the road again. He already had one or two gaffs lined up between Brighton and home base at Worthing. It was not sensible to travel far with August Bank Holiday Races so soon on the calendar.

Steyning cricket fête, 1929.

Joe's gallopers at Steyning, 1929.

Bunny, a servant girl, and Louie Matthews.

Bunny and Henry Lord Leonard leaning against wagon steps.

Bill holding 'Peter', one of his favourite dogs.

Johnny, son of John and Naomi Matthews, sitting on roundabout steps.

Amy (on Right) with her sister-in-law, Naomi Matthews.

John and Naomi Matthews's grave in Brighton. Their children included Clara, Rosie, Beatrice, Ada and Johnny.

Saturday, 20 July, found him in the Shoreham area. By eight in the evening the stuff had already been open for several hours and takings were good – some compensation for the weather which was unpleasantly hot and close. Rain, or King Parney (as showmen irreverently called their enemy) clearly threatened. The pleasure of the evening was suddenly interrupted, and not just by rain ...

It was almost exactly half-past eight when all the tilts billowed like hot-air balloons trying to break away from moorings. Skilfully piled pyramids of swag on spinners and wheel'em-ins swayed, glassware smashed, women screamed.

"It's the end of the world, the end of the world ..." Echoes whispered through the fairground long after people had fled, but the showmen had no time to listen so busy were they tying down tilts and securing lamps. For about fifteen minutes the most extraordinary cyclonic wind and storm raged, accompanied by a tidal wave. Fortunately, it happened at low tide otherwise the death toll and damage would have been enormous. Further east along the coast people lost their lives at Hastings, Folkestone and Southend.[4] Joe's family repaired the storm damage and were soon back in Brighton for the Great August Race Fair. Their advertising among showmen and public poster campaign paid dividends. The splendid array of riding machines which attended included Gray's grand electric scenic railway, Whittle's electric jumpers, Brooklyn Cakewalk and Flying Chairs, Botton's three abreast, Matthews' gallopers, and Sully's and Hammond Brothers'

Chris Hammond and his wife with their juvenile roundabout at Littlehampton.

juvenile roundabouts. Not only the local population but hundreds of Brighton's holiday-makers flocked in to enjoy the fun.[5]

Even after the October Race Meeting was over, Joe spent much time in Brighton that winter. His younger brother, John, had pulled in there for winter months during the last twenty-eight years so that his wife Naomi could be near her mother, old Charity Smith, daughter of William Wilkins the showman who had been killed in a contest on the Racehill in 1869. There was local outcry in January 1930 when Charity, a widow of eighty, was ordered to leave the pitch in Brighton where her caravan had rested for fifty years.[6] No sooner had she settled on another

Joe and daughters in front of his 'Peacock Spinner'.

piece of land close by, when the family was shocked by the sudden death of John Matthews at the age of fifty-three.[7] Charity did not long survive her son-in-law.

So, the Mulo-mush was out again, and tapping. Joe grieved after the death of his brother, but put more energy than ever into the lively touring fair he was creating. His sons and daughters had all but grown up now – the youngest, Beatie, being fifteen. Still Joe held his family together and ruled them with a very firm hand.

The eldest girl, Louie, was twenty-eight in 1930 and had been courted by a fellow-traveller for the past seven years. It was an open secret, of course, that

Harry and Louie were sweet on each other and there was nothing particularly wrong with the young man, but her parents discouraged any marriage plans Louie tried to make. After all, she was a good worker, a second mother to the younger children. She surely had all she could want for, what need to go casting eyes at fellers? Anyway, what sort of future had

Harry Stroud who married Louie Matthews.

Louie, eldest daughter of Joe and Amy Matthews.

Henry, Bill and Joe Matthews after the death of their brother John.

Harry Stroud to offer a wife? Like Joe's boys, he was still travelling with his family and expected to put his all into the collective enterprise with little opportunity to create an independent living for himself.

Henry Francis Stroud was born at the Railway Inn in Earlswood, Surrey, on 10 February 1902. His father was from a fairground family very similar in background, indeed linked in several generations already, to the Matthews clan. Harry's Uncle Charlie married Lydia Bailey, granddaughter of Chewbacca. Harry's grandmother was Martha Deakins whose brother married Lavinia Bushnell, sister of Redshirt's wife.

So how did Harry come to be born in a pub? In 1896 his father had made a decision to quit the travelling life. He was lessee of many fairs in Surrey, Sussex, Hampshire and Kent, a prosperous showman, and immensely proud of his beautiful bride when she arrived at Brentford Church in December 1894 dressed in wide-brimmed hat and hand-made red velvet costume. He felt he was marrying above himself, for Rebecca Augusta Freeman-Biddall was from a travelling tradition more exotic than his own – the circus. Her father's family had been travelling entertainers for over two centuries.

In the 1860s her grandfather had travelled one of the earliest Ghost Illusion Shows as well as a circus. Generations of the Freeman children had been brought up in the circus tradition acquiring conjuring, acrobatic, rope-walking, singing, dancing and instrumentalist skills. Remembering the glories of Barnet Fair in the 1880s, the correspondent of a local newspaper wrote fifty years later:

One recalls the parading of such excellent family artists as the famous Biddall family, with William, expert cornet soloist; John, trombonist; George, double drums; Charles, second cornet; and Rebecca Biddall, with a potpourri of musical juggling with bottles, knives, and tomahawks, assisted by the Misses Polly and Venie Biddall in walking the silver thread.

Becky (Rebecca) partnered her brother Billy in his Mexican knife-throwing act in which she stood motionless against a board while he outlined her body so accurately that the last blades imbedded themselves between her outstretched fingers. The reason she always wore her hair in an unfashionable fringe was her need to disguise the scar left on the occasion when a blade came too close. The wound, though slight, was enough to set spectators screaming as they saw blood spurting from her forehead. There were other occasions when her long hair was singed,

Rebecca and William Biddall in their knife-throwing act c.1890.

even set alight, by flames flaring from the methylated spirits soaked into a sponge fixed on the knife-blades in one part of the act.

Tragedy dissolved the family fortunes. In 1891 their show was on its way to Doncaster Races. Becky was struggling to drive one of the horses and wagons up Gringely Hill, near Gainsborough, when her older sister, Rosanna, jumped off to chock the wheels and tripped in her long skirt. Rosanna was crushed as the wagon rolled backwards.[8] Rosie, their mother,

Biddalls circus and menagerie at Lewes, c1896.

never recovered from the shock of her daughter's death. Her hair fell out and was only just growing back into tight black curls when she herself died ten months later. Her husband did not long outlive her. So, when Becky married, she left a family show which was already disintegrating.

John Stroud provided a luxurious Orton and Spooner wagon for her comfort and in Spring 1896 he felt like a king as he drove it out on to the road on the way to their first gaff of the season. It was a splendid-looking wagon – and all along the way it excited admiration. John felt happy until he overheard an exclamation from the crowd:

"Oh, look! Here come the gypsies. Aren't they interesting?" GYPSIES? John and Becky were furious. How could anyone mistake their magnificent living-carriage for a gypsy vardo?

"I won't have it!" John stormed. "That's decided me. I'm gonner settle down."

True to his word, he had soon negotiated purchase of the *Railway Inn*, which stood next to his sister Lizzie Irvin's yard at Earlswood, but despite his settled address and new occupation he remained lessee of many fairs. Becky also kept close contact with her brothers who were now travelling a Mexican Circus and Bioscope Show.

A photograph of John Stroud sitting between George Taylor and Billy Biddall on the steps of this show was taken at Mitcham Fair just weeks before he died in September 1909. He was only thirty-nine and left Becky with seven children to bring up on her own. She turned to the fairground to find ways of making a living for her family, able to draw on her husband's legacy of leases for annual fairs at Hampton Court, Epsom, Fareham, Bognor, Horsham, Strood, Great Marlow, Wokingham, and Blackwater. She was also lessee of Redhill Sportsground and here in 1910 Uncle Man-Chris Odam admonished her about carrying her takings home late at night.

"I want you to promise me you'll be more careful, my gal," he said. "You don't know what evil folks there is lurking about ready to attack a body for money."

Becky had cause to remember his warning. One evening some months later she heard a newspaper-boy crying through the street:

"Showman murdered! Showman found murdered! Read all about it!" She sent one of the children to buy a copy and learnt that an old man whose identity was as yet unknown had been murdered the night before in Balcombe Road, Horley.

Later came a heavy knock at the door, and the local policeman was there to ask her to go with him to try to put a name to the body. Becky went to the police station and was able to recognise Uncle Man-Chris despite the fact that, as she said, 'his jaw was at the top of his head'. After that she went straight to Aunt Chrissy, his wife, and tried to comfort her.

A local labourer was brought to court charged with the murder. However, so rudimentary was forensic science at this time that Dr Willcox, who was simultaneously working on the Crippen case, was unable to distinguish between human and animal bloodstains. The suspect was discharged and the murderer never convicted.

Rebecca Stroud's set of Chairoplanes.

When her two eldest sons went off to the War in 1914 Becky took her younger children to London, wintering in her wagon at Customs House, Poplar. After 1918 she bought a fine set of Chairoplanes from Charles Abbot and toured with these through the southern counties, frequently meeting up with Biddall's Mexican Circus and another famous Wild West Show, the Shufflebottoms. This show provided another link between Harry and his future bride.

The founder of the Shufflebottoms was an American, Texas Bill – sharp-shooter, knife-thrower, rope-artist, and rough-rider – who came over to England with the first Buffalo Bill Circus. He settled, married, and started a circus of his own – just as Harry's cousins, the Hannefords, reversed the process by setting off for the

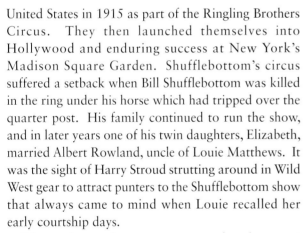

Wally Shufflebottom and Harry Stroud.

Harry Stroud on one of Joe's engines.

United States in 1915 as part of the Ringling Brothers Circus. They then launched themselves into Hollywood and enduring success at New York's Madison Square Garden. Shufflebottom's circus suffered a setback when Bill Shufflebottom was killed in the ring under his horse which had tripped over the quarter post. His family continued to run the show, and in later years one of his twin daughters, Elizabeth, married Albert Rowland, uncle of Louie Matthews. It was the sight of Harry Stroud strutting around in Wild West gear to attract punters to the Shufflebottom show that always came to mind when Louie recalled her early courtship days.

Throughout the summer months they met regularly at various gaffs, lingering after closing-time to chat in the shadows until the stillness was shattered by Joe's shrill whistle sounded twice to summon his family into the wagons. She and Harry discovered other ways of communicating too. Letters addressed to 'Mrs Cook' and 'Mr Wright' and marked *Poste restante* were sent to certain towns and villages about to receive a visit from a fair. The letters to 'Mr Wright', written in carefully rounded script invariably began,

Dear Harry,
I hope this finds you as it leaves me …

One day early in 1931 a letter arrived for Louie with exciting news. Harry had been saving his money and now he had a chance to buy a home for them both. There was a man at Lewisham who had offered him a second-hand Tilling-Stevens bus suitable for living in. Would she like to come and inspect it? Poor Louie took this at more than its face value. She thought it was the message she had been awaiting for years. Without alerting anyone who might have tried to stop her, she packed a suitcase with all her worldly possessions and set off supposedly to get married.

Harry was horrified. Of course he wanted to marry her, he muttered, but not like this. He wanted everything done properly; no question of a broomstick wedding as far as he was concerned. He would get together a home for them both and then approach Joe for his blessing. Louie went back to face the wrath of her family. Soon afterwards, with Joe's grudging consent, Harry married his sweetheart and their first child was born in February 1932.

Louie's brother Tom was particularly interested in the arrival of the new baby and most of all anxious to know what she would be called. He had almost completed his winter task of repainting the horses on the gallopers; all but one had its name in scrolled letters round its neck. Most bore names of members

Louie with engagement ring.

Amy, her son, Tom, and a 'little servant girl' (kitchen tent in background).

Below: Harry and Louie's first home, a Tilling-Stevens bus, 1934.

Servant girl fondling the dog.

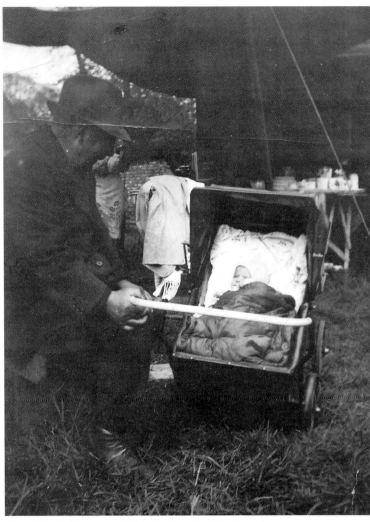

Joe with his first grandchild, Barbara Louisa Stroud.

Roundabout before refurbishment. Matthews and Stroud families. Joe's brother John on left.

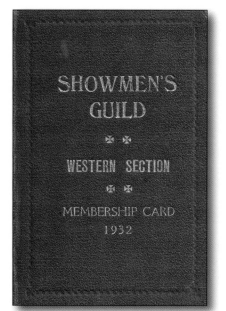
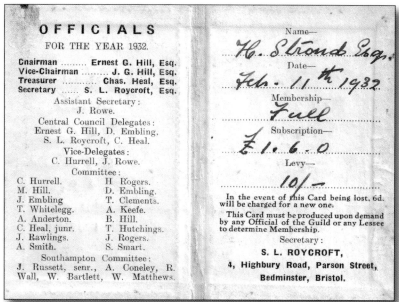

Harry's Showmen's Guild Membership Card.

of the family and the last had been reserved for Joe and Amy's first grandchild. However, as the fond new parents dithered and could not make up their minds, Tom started painting. First he wrote 'Baby' and then, paintbrush in hand, strode to Louie's bus to ask what should follow. "Oh! just make it 'Baby Babs,'" said Harry, and the name was adopted for the horse and the little girl who was later christened Barbara Louisa.

That winter, while the family were pulled in at Gosport, the gallopers had once more been completely transformed. Its tubular metal shafts had already been replaced by shiny spiralled brass rods with special acorn heads supplied by the firm of Vospers. Now the roundabout received its crowning glory in the shape of carved domes and droppers to embellish the top rounding boards. Joe and one of his sons travelled to Margate to buy them from

Whayman & Hastings (Canterbury) roundabout which burnt down and supplied drops and rounding boards to Joe's gallopers.

Whaymans and Hastings whose roundabout had burnt out at Dreamland Park.

After Tom repainted them, the domes were fitted with cut glass mirrors bearing the initials 'J.M.'

'Southdown', writing for the World's Fair, visited Portslade in May 1932 and found Joe's family open on the Quay with 'undoubtedly one of the prettiest sets of three-abreasts in the country'. The roundabout was brilliantly illuminated by power being generated by the Fowler locomotive Wanderer, and nearby Sunny South was busily engaged driving a set of chairoplanes at top speed. Other amusements included Matthews' Park Swings, hooplas, rings and darts stalls. There were several sideshows such as Captain Davenport's Go-Man-Vu-La dried up man, the Giant Rat Exhibition and the Lobster-clawed Girl. Clarence Tattersall was showing Harold Pyott as 'Tiny Tim' standing only twenty three inches high (over twelve inches less than the renowned General Tom Thumb.) Madame Eugenie represented The Great French Theatre in a tasteful posing show in which, it was claimed, 'cleanliness predominated throughout'.[9]

Despite the Depression local communities made the best hay possible when the sun shone. Several times that year Joe returned to open on Baltic Wharf, Portslade, and the townsfolk invariably turned out to support him. In August the usually peaceful Sussex village of Steyning staged a grand carnival: a fancy dress parade, prehistoric tableaux, decorated lorries, tug-o-war, bunny wheel, London Bridge, name the cockerel – and Joe's roundabout at the heart of the bright pageantry.[10] The beautiful ride and smart appearance of all their equipment now made the

Above: Family group in front of refurbished gallopers. Harry holds his baby daughter.

Right: Joe, Amy and their nine sons and daughters, Steyning, 1932.

Below: Matthews family grouped on gallopers at Steyning, 1932. Joe with granddaughter.

Above left: Joe's set of chairoplanes.

Above right: Chairoplanes. Bill Matthews in centre.

Left: Chairoplanes being driven at full speed by *Sunny South.*

it into a temporary amusement park. Sheltered behind hoardings posted with advertisements for the current review at the Hippodrome, the tober was well-lit and inviting.[11]

Apart from Marshall Hill's Noah's Ark, foremost among the attractions was Joe's set of gallopers. Young Joe had taken over responsibility for the centre engine, while Tom and Bill took the 'doings' from the riders. 'Adagio', reporting for *World's Fair*, 3 December 1932, noted:

'By far the most striking thing about this ride is the magnificent examples of the painter's art which adorn it. Painted on the ride are many fine pictures depicting life in the jungle, all kinds of wild beasts and they are all painted with such skill, and such attention to detail that they show the touch of a real artist. Above the organ on the top are a set of wonderful, hand-painted

Matthews' family fair a welcome addition to any local celebration.

At Chichester Fair in 1932 King Parney 'reigned' with a vengeance, ruining the showmen's harvest. Winter presented a bleak prospect until Joe found a way to augment the family income. Instead of pulling in after the backend run, he rented a pitch from Messrs Hill Brothers who had cleared a piece of waste ground in Commercial Road, Portsmouth, and turned

Sunny South photographed on Upper Shoreham Road, Shoreham c1935.

pictures. This is a real novelty in riding-machine decoration, being none other than life-like portraits of famous film stars. On casually asking Bill Matthews who the artist was, and expecting to hear the name of a well-known showland painter, I received the astonishing reply: "Oh, Tom." "Tom? Tom who?" I questioned in perplexity. "Why, Tom Matthews, my brother," laughed Bill. "And here he is," he said, as Tom wended his way towards us through the lines of galloping horses.'

Bill then led his new friend to inspect the three traction engines and a rather special two-and-a-half ton packing truck – special because Tom had been to work with his paintbrush on this too. A Roman chariot raced along one side, its horses about to career out of the picture; on the other side were eight illustrated verses of *Widecombe Fair*. Positioned prominently on the tober, this truck drew crowds and came to be regarded as a show in itself.

Before the family was ready to take to the road again next April, the Boys had completely overhauled *The Wanderer*, using no fewer than forty gold leaf books in its renovation.[12] Baltic Wharf, Portslade, was their first port of call and business was good. They opened at West Worthing for Easter before moving on to Brighton for the May Races Fair. The

showmen were amazed to find that, almost while their backs were turned, a new town had sprung up within ten minutes' walk of the Race Hill fairground, with hundreds of new houses being built since the previous year.[13] A major attraction at this fair was Bob Gandy's circus. Unfortunately, the Big Top could not withstand a sudden squall that blew up on Thursday night and had to be pulled down in a hurry, losing the owner a night's business. Joe's roundabout also suffered, with the top tilt getting badly torn.[14]

Joe's younger brothers set up business in Worthing, 1920s.

Joe's youngest brother Henry Lord Leonard Matthews standing next to one of George Baker's Fodens.

Joe's two wagons mounted back-to-back on a single chassis.

Out came the treadle sewing machine and Amy sat in the middle of the field mending the canvas.

The family kept mostly to the Sussex coast that summer, making an extended stay at Newhaven in July before travelling to Portslade and on to Brighton for August Bank Holiday. On one of these journeys a policeman cautioned Joe against pulling more than three loads behind one traction engine. Joe pondered the problem before setting the Boys to work. No sooner had they drawn on to the highway again than they were challenged by the same police officer.

"I'm sorry Mr Matthews, but I did warn you about pulling four loads behind one engine, and now it is my duty to …"

"Wait a minute," says Joe. "How many wheels would you expect to find under four trucks?"

"Sixteen?" suggested the policeman, puzzled.

"Right," says Joe. "Now count the wheels under my loads."

There were but twelve. The family's two full size living-wagons had been mounted back to back on a huge single chassis and they travelled thus until backend.

On another occasion Joe's youngest brother was driving a traction engine when pulled up by a policeman demanding to see his driving licence. After a little search he was able to hand the document to the officer. The latter took a long time studying its contents. Suddenly he made up his mind and moved with alacrity.

"Thank you, Sir. Sorry to have delayed your journey," he said, with a smart salute. It sometimes helped to have forenames such as Henry *Lord* Leonard.

With his two brothers, four sons and son-in-law all pulling their weight, Joe was able to travel a very respectable fair. There was the roundabout, chairoplanes, park swings, spinner, darts, rings, touch-'ems, coconut shies, rifle shooters and wheel-'em-ins

– but still room for something more. Faster, more up-to-date rides were coming into the business. In July 1933 Joe purchased a dodgem track. The cars were of Lusse make, fitted with Leyland electric motors and coming complete with trucks and packing on three loads. They were equipped with amplified music.[15] Amy and Annie, attractive twins just approaching their twenty-first birthday, liked nothing better than to sit in the pay-box checking up, working the switchboard and changing the records.

The weather was lovely that autumn, enticing large crowds to visit Sloe Fair at Chichester and the enormous fair that followed at Winchester. Here twelve big machines opened for a nine days run.[16] Many people stood admiring the bright rides, listening to the music, thrusting their hands deep into empty pockets. Money was scarce; the winter months

The Touch'ems with (left to right) Beatie, Chap, Harry, Mabel Cothard, Amy.

Henry Lord Leonard Matthews minding the juvenile roundabout.

Rosie, Beatie, Amy and Annie posing next to the Wheel-'em-in.

The Touch'ems with five girls including (right to left) May Stroud, Louie and Rosie.

Above: Henry Lord Leonard minding Joe's Park Swings at Shoreham.

Left: Posing in front of the Dart Stall – the seven girls include Louie, Amy, two Rosies and two Beaties.

Below: Henry Lord Leonard and Bill Matthews, sitting on dodgems with chavvies and jukels.

Pedlar's Certificate envelope.

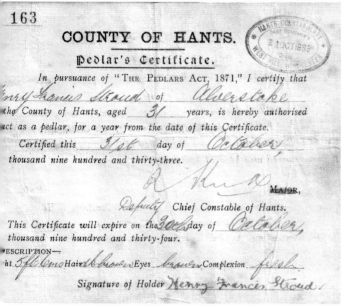

Harry's Pedlar's Certificate, 1933.

threatened to be lean. Joe's former ground at Portsmouth was not available because of nearby building operations. As soon as Winchester fair was over, Louie's husband took himself along to the Chief Constable's Office to apply for a pedlar's certificate. Pride was humbled in coming weeks as Harry walked from door to door selling cheap pens and notepaper, but wife and baby ate without his getting into debt and he had enough money for petrol to get himself on to the road the following Spring.

With his whole family feeling the pinch, Joe determined on an early start for the 1934 season by opening at Portslade on 9 March. A cold east wind meant that business was quiet.[17] Easter at Glebe Road, West Worthing, was scarcely any better, but things improved when the fair returned again to Portslade in April.[18] Crowds were still thronging the ground after eleven o'clock on a Saturday evening

Vicar taking money on Park Swings, possibly at Shoreham.

Below: Portslade – fairground scene including swings.

when Joe was compelled to close down rather than risk conflict with the authorities. He had learned that it was better to work with the establishment than to antagonise it. After all, wasn't he a man with a reputation to protect? Regular benefactor of local charities; a man whose name blazed on brightly coloured posters along the south coast throughout the summer months. He was well pleased with his lot.

Journalist Alfred Keeping conveyed this feeling when he wrote about Joe in *World's Fair*, 7 July 1934:

MIDNIGHT ON BRIGHTON DOWNS

"What better life could anyone wish for?" so remarked Mr Joseph Matthews to me as the clock was striking the midnight hour when he came outside his well-fitted-up mess tent to bid me goodnight on Brighton Race Course Fair Ground. I had previously enjoyed his hospitality in the tent adjoining his living carriage, and had had a most interesting chat after the show was over. What a wealth of experience Mr Matthews has had in his lengthy career of showlife, to be sure. His reminiscences would fill pages.

Outside the tent were members of Mr Matthews' family seated round a coke fire. It was a beautiful moonlit night, with a gentle breeze blowing the solitude of the Downs, the arduous day's toil over and all was now peace and quiet, with roundabout, chairs, stalls, living carriages silhouetted against a glorious night sky. I felt quite reluctant to leave this nocturnal showman's retreat and, as I wended my way homeward over the moonlit Downs and later gave a glance back at the peaceful scene depicting Showland at rest, I could not help agreeing with Mr Matthews' remark: "What better life could anyone wish for?"

A reader might well be charmed by such a romantic scene, but there were other, less attractive, facets of a traveller's life. Harry, the winter before, had walked over twenty miles a day trying to sell pens and paper, and on occasion chamois leathers packed in a suitcase with cabbage leaves to keep them moist.

Other travellers had made a living by 'logging'. They bought a small copse of standing wood and parked their living-wagons close by. Having felled the young trees, the men brought trunks and branches back to their portable saw-bench and, as damp November turned sharp with cold, their numb fingers had to slide the timber against unguarded blades. Woe betide he whose concentration wavered. An impatient shove of an intransigent log resulted in fingers lost.

Every member of the family except the baby was involved in the work; the boys using bill-hooks to split larger logs, or helping the girls who, with small hatchets, were chopping logs into kindling pieces. Even small chavvies helped with making these into little round bundles known as 'pimps'. First, they gathered the kindling pieces and packed them upright

Matthews and Studt families at Poole Fair, November 1932 (from left to right) Mrs Matthews (from Wales), Amy Matthews, Mrs Charlie Studt, Amy, Beatie (holding Barbara), Annie, a girl Matthews and a boy Stevens. In front are Mrs Studt's children.

Henry Chipperfield (of Fleet, Hants) and his family.

Dolly Smart and her family on wagon steps.

into a tin can that had been cut down and nailed securely by its base to a flat log. When the can was full, the chavvies twisted a length of wire round the sticks to hold them together, lifted the bundle out and threw it on to a pile.

Meanwhile, what were the women doing? Near Christmas they might be turning the wood shavings into artificial chrysanthemums or making holly wreaths for sale. Apart from logging, the men also turned their hands to making pegs, stools, small besoms – traditional Romany crafts. Yet, call a showman a gypsy and don't stop running until you reach home! There was no greater insult in their vocabulary.

Hereditary showmen were a race apart; different from flatties, and a cut above all other travellers on the road – at least according to their own proud reckoning. Joe Matthews and old Andrew Smith,

claiming ability to trace their respective families back more than a couple of hundred years, boasted of generations who had made their living at fairs.

"And none of OUR lot were ever hedge-mumpers or needies," each declared, glaring at the other.

Even when Joe's family got by in winter months without resort to other than fairground jobs, they were certainly never idle. Always there was some work of repair, restoration, building or decoration which needed doing. The girls, in addition to regular domestic chores such as washing, cleaning, shopping and cooking, turned their hands to sewing and crochet work, producing bedspreads and tablecloths finely wrought with complex pineapple patterns. They were always on the lookout for dark-printed material suitable for making pinafores.

Winter months, however spent, were something of a trial. Travelling along the south coast in summer

Dolly Smart with her six children.

Group including twins, Beatie, and cousin Rosie.

provided joyful contrast. The youngsters loved swimming and at Littlehampton, Worthing, Shoreham, Portslade and Newhaven, as soon as they had pulled in and built up, if the sun was shining, off they all skipped to the beach. Never lonely, they met up with special companions from other travelling families at the bigger gaffs and there were cousins who came simply to enjoy a change from their own part of the country. In towns where the fair stayed regularly every summer locals greeted them as returning friends and shed tears as they waved them goodbye again. One such was Chris Wickenden, son of 'Singing Charley Lee', who looked forward excitedly to the Matthews' fair visiting his home town of Newhaven every year. His special pal was young Johnny Matthews, Joe's nephew, and every time they came the two lads would spend time together.

Years later he reminisced: 'I remember polishing the brass on the *Wanderer* with young Johnny and when I was doing it I felt as if I was as near to heaven as a young boy could get … There was a pub close by our old cottage in Essex Place called *The Blacksmith's Arms*. This was a great favourite with the Matthews Boys, and after a Sunday night in the *Blacksmiths'* they would sometimes bring in a couple of bottles of beer and have some supper with us, and sit and yarn about old times, which of course they'd been doing all the evening in the pub, which was Dad's local. It was by the riverside and it was a very happy pub.

Travelling chavvies – the group includes Matthews and Coles families.

Chavvies in front of a round stall.

Right: ' The chavvies were never lonely'.

Didley's Annie and her brother. 'Didley', or William Matthews (1896-1946), was a grandson of Chewbacca's eldest son, James.

Left: Louie as little mother to her younger siblings.

On the beach after a dip.

A chavvy calling Bob, the dog.

Beatie Matthews and her cousin Rosie baby-sitting.

Rosie, a friend, Louie and Amy.

'Young John and myself would be outside sitting on the railing on the riverbank with crisps and lemonade supplied by the Boys. I used to like getting him to tell me about the places he had been to, and I used to tell him about our town and the harbour. I envied John like hell, when I thought he is actually part of it all – the gallopers, the engines, especially big *Wanderer*, in fact the whole thing. I remember one time, after the fair had moved out, I wandered over to the fairground (in New Road at that time) and went into the ground looking at all the traces left behind, all the darker green patches of grass where the side stuff and the rides had been. I went and stood on the large patch where the gallopers had stood, looking at the ashes from the centre engine, and I imagined it all back again, in my mind. I could hear the organ, playing again *The Blue Danube* waltz which I doted on as a kid, a tune that seemed as if it had been written especially for Matthews's Gaudin organ with its wonderful lilt. I remember it was a lovely summer day, I was alone in the field, just moving about. I looked up at the Downs and knew that the fair was somewhere on the other side of that range of hills, and I suddenly felt quite forlorn.'

The 1934 season was a triumph for Joe. Apart from three Brighton Race Hill Fairs, there were stays at Shoreham, Portslade, Newhaven, Lewes and two visits to Uckfield. The second was for the town's carnival in September. The amusements were built up in a meadow near the railway station and the rides were motley thronged with Roundheads, Cavaliers, Courtiers, Kings, Chinamen and Clowns, all waging confetti war and filling the air with bright streamers.[19]

Beatie, Cousin Rosie, and Amy sitting on the steps of the gallopers.

Sliding down the bank at Portslade.

Annie, Amy, Beatie behind the carved wagon.

Louie sitting behind the carved wagon.

All through the summer Tom had been working on the dodgems, which he had almost re-painted in time for Sloe Fair. Showmen pulled into a convenient place in Chichester a day or two beforehand knowing that the gates were locked to prevent them entering the fairfield before seven o'clock in the morning of 20 October. The quality of their pitch and therefore the size of their takings depended on being first in the race to the tober.

On one occasion many years before, Dicky Wall and Joe had both chosen to pull in to the *Black Boy Inn* yard to await the vital moment for departure. In the bar Dicky boasted about the speed and power of his Burrell.

"You won't see the going of me," he said to Joe, who had only his Tasker to compete with.

"Go on, I shall be with you all the way," said Joe.

Dicky did not see him fix a chain from the three-tonner to the back of his Burrell and could not conceal his amazement when Joe stayed on the road just behind him and followed him closely into the fairground.

As time went on, three families – Coles, Walls, and Matthewses – worked out their strategy each year with military precision. Their loads were drawn up in three lines in the market place with the traction engines fretting to move off. The trick consisted in getting up sufficient steam to pass through the gate first. Blows and cussing accompanied the struggle. Then, some years, even the first drivers to arrive at the ground were confounded. Men the previous night had surreptitiously carried poles into the town and thrown them over the walls to stake their pitches.

Building-up involved much frantic activity – little time to look about you. On the other hand, who could resist downing tools to go and stare at the sight of two travellers erecting their separate wheel-'em-ins on the same spot? It happened at Sloe Fair. Two showmen claiming the same pitch and refusing to give way – hammering in their stakes, bolting on their shutters. setting out their swag until they had both put up one half of their 'round-'un'. Then, no longer on speaking terms and determined to ignore each other, at opening time they stood back-to-back minding their own business for the duration of the fair.

Joe had done much to introduce order into the letting procedures at Sloe Fair and in particular was responsible for compiling an acceptable tariff of charges. In 1934 for the second year running the weather was fine. Being a one-day event, an early opening time was possible, although not until half-past two were crowds large enough to justify starting up the big rides.

Street fair at Petworth. Young Joe Matthews building up his coconut shy.

Petworth Winter Fair on 20 November was the last gaff in what had been a mighty strenuous season. Joe had been on the road building up, pulling down and moving on ever since the beginning of March when he had opened at Portslade. He had made several return visits to what had become a favourite venue of his. On his last visit he had been disappointed to hear that Portslade's Baltic Wharf was about to be converted into a landing dock and would no longer be available to travelling showmen.[20] It marked the end of an era.

Gloom settled over the family after they pulled into winter quarters at the Hermitage, Emsworth. Joe was ill. Just before Christmas he went into Havant hospital for a stomach operation, coming back thankfully to the wagon early in the new year.

Despite their anxiety, the Boys continued to busy themselves re-painting and refurbishing the tackle, hoping that once out on the road at the end of March their father might regain something of his old vitality. On the other hand, Amy worried lest Joe be taken ill again at a distance from the doctors who had charge of his case. Should she stay behind to look after him when the new season started? She had no time to reach a decision. On 13 March Joe died.

Dozens of black hired motor cars conveyed travellers in solemn procession to the cemetery for his funeral. So long did the cortege take to wind itself

Funeral of Joe Matthews, March 1935.

Floral wreaths at Joe's funeral.

123

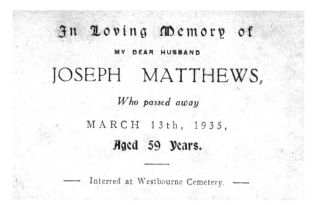

In Loving Memory of

MY DEAR HUSBAND

JOSEPH MATTHEWS,

Who passed away

MARCH 13th, 1935,

Aged 59 Years.

—— Interred at Westbourne Cemetery. ——

Memorial card for Joe.

down the country lane that the interment ceremony had to begin before the last car had deposited its passengers. Hundreds of people had gathered to pay their respects.

Worthing Herald announced:

Joe Matthews, happiest and politest of showmen, born into the life of merry-go rounds and coconut shies, is dead. Joe's death has robbed Sussex of a familiar figure known in every town on the South Coast where his fairground has given happy hours to countless children. His death has meant the passing of another phase in the life of Matthews' Fun Fair. Joe was born in showbusiness. His father, grandfather and great-grandfather were all showmen, and they all travelled through the county.

Joe Matthews was known particularly well to Shoreham where he did a great deal for the Old Folks' Dinner Fund. He took part in many of the outdoor events in the town. It is said that he was the first man to introduce electricity to Worthing. "My father had his own plant, and I believe at the Norfolk Hotel, in Chapel Road, he had the first electric light erected. It was an arc-lamp and caused a great deal of talk at the time."

In a week the show opens again. His sons will carry on.

Grief dwells with open face among travellers. The show went on. Sons and daughters making extra efforts to reassure Amy that all was well, but no one pretended that things could ever be the same without Joe at the helm. Although no longer able to use Baltic Wharf, they still opened the 1935 season at Portslade on 29 March.

Amy was alone in the Darts Stall that afternoon. A little group of children walked past, with eyes for nothing but the roundabout.

"I s'pose now Mr Matthews isn't here,' said one to the other, "there won't be any more free rides."

Amy ran to her son, telling him to announce that the roundabout was just starting up for the first ride and that, as usual, all children were invited to climb on free of charge. Soon *Sussex by the Sea* resounded from the Gaudin. Horses rose and fell. Children waved. And grown-ups wept.

Joe Matthews.

Chapter Twelve
JOE'S BOYS

Joe Matthews, senior, has gone to his rest, but he leaves behind a large, capable, and hard-working family which will, one prognosticates, carry on the 'show' and worthily uphold the Matthews' tradition.

(*World's Fair*, 23 March 1935)

Amy had one remedy for grief, hard work. Her sons and daughters strove to keep up with her, out of consideration for their mother holding in check their own natural impetuosity and impatience with each other. No one was allowed any time to mope. Before Easter the Boys had constructed a new wooden fit-up kitchen to replace the tent in which Amy and the Girls had previously done the cooking.

They hurled themselves into the seasonal round, Easter at Worthing, Brighton in June and August, in July a new site at Newhaven situated on the main road near the harbour gates, then on to Shoreham Flower Show and the local Police Sports' Day. In intervals between opening they re-layed and strengthened the flooring frames of the dodgem track. The result was what was described in August as one of the best pleasure fairs seen at Brighton for years, with the Boys earning credit for the way they laid out the ground.[1]

After August Bank Holiday the family split to allow one section to go to Shoreham while the dodgems, chairoplanes and some sideshows opened at Worthing Flower Show. Louie's husband, Harry, dressed in his 'whites' and with a cheeky line of patter, presented a new auto-cricket game – a great hit with sporting fans eager to participate in his top-score competitions. There were also the sensational Wall of Death Riders, presented by Elias Harris, who included in their act the Lion on the Wall.

The family reunited on Shoreham's Adur Memorial Ground where the Boys' enterprise again drew the crowds. They overcame the difficulty of the bank surrounding the field by building up a slope consisting of railway sleepers and blocks supported on a trolley truck in the centre. Next, they constructed a triple-entrance trellis arch picked out in bright lights to beckon people in from the main road. Thirty or forty cars parked outside on the opening night augured success for the rest of their stay. One evening's takings of the rides, amounting to £8.5s., was handed over to the Old Folks' Dinner

Fund with assurances that the family intended to maintain the tradition founded by Joe.[2]

Joseph Norfolk Matthews, striving to carry on just as Joe would have wished, was not always comfortable under his father's mantle. On 26 June, while on the road to Hailsham, the family was stopped at Ringles Cross by police who eyed their heavy loads with clear displeasure. A whole series of

Joe's boys.

summonses ensued. Henry Lord Leonard was charged with driving a steam vehicle with three trailers attached, plus a water tank ten feet long, eight feet wide and two feet deep, and around the tank more than a ton of coal. Joseph testified that they were carrying two hundred gallons of water and fifteen hundredweight of coal, quantities just sufficient for their journey. When it transpired that no one in court could swear to the correct unladen weight of the engine concerned, the case was dismissed. "It really is a most confusing vehicle," the prosecution sighed. Later, fines were imposed on Joseph and his brother Bill for driving heavy locomotives without the necessary attendants and on young Amy for driving a light locomotive without a driving licence.[3]

In September amidst stormy weather the family made a prolonged stay at Shoreham to enable the Boys to replace the wire netting on the frame sections of the dodgems with new wire of a more durable gauge, and fit up a quantity of lamps they had just bought from Brighton Corporation. After Sloe Fair they journeyed to Winchester and Poole before returning to Petworth Winter Fair.

Alfred Keeping described the event in *World's Fair*, 23 November 1935. "Making my way to the Market Place, I noted all the wagons and trucks had been drawn up alongside the entrance streets while great credit is due to J. Matthews & Sons for the manner in which the rides and shows had been arranged in the Square. They had certainly made the most of the ground space there.

"Business was quite steady, despite the unsettled weather and it so happened on my visit that they had arranged to give the whole of the takings from the gallopers and radio cars towards the Petworth Church Spire Fund. Everything in the fair was well lighted, while the presence of streamers, balloons, etc. was proof that the carnival spirit was well to the fore. In fact, it was all that could be desired to brighten up a dull November day."

At the beginning of December the family opened at Fratton Road, Portsmouth, for a two months' run which left the Boys just six weeks to carry out their next refurbishment schemes. They reconstructed and extended the top of the dodgems, at the same time enlarging and rounding off the ends of the flooring to eliminate the possibility of cars jamming or interlocking. The four brothers made all the woodwork and joists, even going so far as to make the iron angle plates themselves. Tom painted the recently-acquired packing van and in April, just before opening up for the 1936 season, was busy fitting mirrors in his mother's brand new living-

Amy's new living-wagon made by Ellis of Chertsey.

wagon. Bought from its manufacturers, Ellis of Chertsey, it came complete with stove, cooker, two bedrooms, cupboards, mantle, and oriel windows of diamond leaded glass.[4]

Amy proudly set out her ornaments, green fluted vase in the centre of the mantelpiece, flanked by two sets of green china rabbits and a pair of tiny glass violet vases; a large cut glass punch bowl on the chest of drawers.

Amy's modern trailer was but one sign of changes on the tober, where new, faster rides were being developed. Keeping pace with fashion, the Boys sold their chairoplanes to showman, Len Buckland, and in its place bought a smaller and speeded-up version of a switchback. The first of these new rides, known as a Noah's Ark, had been introduced to the fairground by William Wilson and appeared at Mitcham Fair in August 1930. It featured at least eighty animals – giraffes, camels, stags, cockerels, pelicans, peacocks, and (wrote the *World's Fair* correspondent):

"*You sit on the back of one and then you are whirled around first slowly, then at breakneck speed, and you are taken over innumerable hills, up and down, and up again – and round and round all the time at nearly 20 m.p.h.*"

The people of Brighton had their chance to experience these thrills when G.A.Whittle brought his Noah's Ark to the August Races Fair in 1932.

As soon as the Boys took possession of their machine, out came Tom's paintbrushes revelling in the scope for more and fiercer beasts to prowl through wilder jungles. While he worked, his four-year-old niece danced on the steps like a young parader.[5]

The refurbishment programme was never-ending. Early in 1937 the animal mounts on the Ark were fitted up with shiny chromium metal and motorcycles were added. All the carvings on the gallopers were repainted and gilded in rainbow colours. More

Wanderer at West Worthing, Amy's wagon in background.

Barbara on top step of Amy's new wagon.

Barbara and her cousin, Josie Sully, in front of Joe's Foden PN7084.

carvings were fixed between the dodgem uprights, its tilt extended, new cars bought. During their stay at Worthing over Easter the Boys were still busy wiring strip lighting round the track.[6] The equipment was thus brought into tip-top condition in time for the special coronation fairs at Crowborough in April and Farnham Park in May.

No visit was made to Brighton Races in June because the ground had been taken for car-parking.[7] Arrangements were later made to hold fairs a little distance from the course, separated from it by a roadway, but the gatherings never regained their former popularity.

To all appearances the firm of J. Matthews & Sons was thriving. Joe's sons and daughters had carried on working harder than ever after their father died, but without his restraining influence the domestic group began to split at the seams. Trouble arose, naturally enough, when one by one siblings introduced marriage partners into the circle. Brothers and brothers-in-law did not always see eye to eye about allocation of pitches. There were bitter rows about who should be allowed to build up where. In July 1937 Harry and Louie left the clan, announcing in the *World's Fair* that 'After many years continuous touring with J. Matthews & Sons, Mr and Mrs Harry Stroud are now negotiating their own bookings.'[8] The other three married daughters soon did likewise, which left the Boys, their wives, and one sister to travel under the old name together with three members of the older generation: Joe's widow, Amy, and Joe's two brothers, William and Henry.

They continued to adapt their equipment, buying a powerful army lorry capable of taking a greater load than the big traction engines as well as driving the lights of the Noah's Ark. They fitted a new tube up the centre of the gallopers and purchased additional books of music for the organ: *Pennies from Heaven*, *The Fleet's in Port Again*, and *Head over Heels*.[9] Tom took charge of the Noah's Ark when the fair opened, his sister sat in the paybox of the dodgems, and Johnny acted as centre-engine driver of the gallopers. When the roundabout takings included any farthings, these were always handed to Johnny to toss into a water-tank under the engine. There the coins remained in what was referred to as 'Johnny's Money Box' until the end of the season, when he retrieved them to spend on some special treat.

At Shoreham in September 1937 the Boys carried out a thorough re-painting of the dodgem cars in brilliant colour designs of red and green on cream background, complete with scrollwork and registration number plates on the back of each car. They re-covered the bass and kettledrums of the

Ruby, Annie Bond's first child, c1938.

Johnny's 'Money-box', a water tank under the engine appropriately named *Dollar Princess*.

Joe's Noah's Ark with Tom's paintings around the top. Two of Harry's daughters and his Vauxhall 12 car are in the foreground.

Beatie Coneley and her daughter Amy on the Isle of Wight, July 1938.

Gaudin organ and added a lively march to its repertoire.[10]

Next, they opened at Horsham where they left the gallopers in store while they completed a brief engagement at Smith's Field, Burgess Hill. Then they picked up the gallopers again en route for Petworth. Nights were drawing in by Sloe Fair time, and Bill fitted a pair of car headlights to the Burrell engine plate in place of the brass oil lamps.[11] The 1937 season was rounded off at a new ground near Fratton Railway Bridge in Goldsmith Avenue.

1938 saw no slackening in the pace of life. Before April the Boys had carved and fitted new top rounding boards on the Noah's Ark, and Tom had decorated the front with a gigantic picture of the hold-up of the Deadwood Coach. They opened at the Adur Memorial Ground, Shoreham, for Easter and then on to Crowborough, Bexhill, Newhaven, Lewes, Horsham, Lancing, Shoreham and Findon. Steyning carnival followed the day after Findon Fair. The rides had to be pulled down during the night, transported, and built up ready to open the next afternoon. Then they travelled on to Wisborough Green, Petworth, Havant, Chichester, and back to Petworth again before concluding the season at Portsmouth.

At the start of the 1939 season Joe's Boys were working really well together, putting hearts and might

into the business. They opened at Portslade on 13 March on a site adjoining Tandy's laundry. On the second day of the fair a 7 h.p. Burrell traction engine that they had just bought was towed in. Before nightfall the Boys had partly dismantled it and started on the job of tyring its wheels.[12]

They used sections of tyres from wheels that had first to be sawn through, stretched, and finally drilled and bolted to the rims of the engine wheels. Knowing the work had to be completed before their next move, Joseph worked through the night by the aid of flood lamps.[13]

The Savage centre engine of Joe's gallopers.

Building up Joe's gallopers. Henry and three Chaps are standing on parts of the park swings. In the background is Joe's Burrell, *Sunny South*.

Many showmen had already changed over from traction engines to lorries. At a recent Sloe Fair the brothers had counted only thirteen traction engines on the ground as opposed to twenty-six petrol-driven vehicles. Their roundabout had been the only set of gallopers present, too, and it had not shown up well against faster rides. Henceforth, when the family attended smaller gaffs, they left the gallopers behind.

Heavy rain before Easter caused terrible problems when building up at Shoreham. On arriving, the Boys found it practically impossible to move their large engines over the marshy ground until they laid down railway sleepers and brought wire hawsers into play. The whole family had just been laid low with

influenza and their sufferings were compounded when three chaps, whom they had generously retained over the winter months, upped and left when most needed.[14]

The family struggled through, and onto Crowborough, and then to Lewes where they opened on Race Hill with the Noah's Ark, dodgems, and sideshows. A reporter called to interview Mrs Amy Matthews about the special benefit night that had raised £10.17s.6d. for the Victoria Hospital Fund. Curious, he peered into a packing truck and caught sight of Tom, busily painting more top roundings for the Ark.[15] Before returning to Lewes in July they visited Rushlake Green, Shoreham, Storrington,

Horsham, Forest Row, and afterwards took in Cross-in-Hand British Legion Fête, Lancing Regatta, and Shoreham Flower Show.[16] What money they earned was ploughed straight back into the business. They bought a new striped tilt for the dodgem track, re-painted several trucks, extended the multicoloured lighting on the roundings of the Ark to the top of the four flagstaffs above its entrance. Tom constructed a mechanical device to operate the lights with the motion of the machine. The effect was dazzling – not that there was much future for dazzling lights on the fairfield in the next few years![17]

On 2 September 1939 the *World's Fair* reported that owing to the general political situation J. Matthews & Sons were remaining at Shoreham until further notice. By the following week they had been closed down by A.R.P. regulations. Enforced 'leisure' enabled them to finish varnishing the rounding boards and to change over tyres from solids to pneumatics to comply with new rules. Although they had a number of tyres, they had difficulty in getting the hubs to fit and travelled miles by car to various manufacturers and dealers to find the right ones.

In the second week of war they moved to Steyning, parking the living-wagons near the football ground while the Boys used their skill with heavy lorries in A.R.P. work. The loads were pulled into a meadow known as the Copse where, after all the frantic activity of previous months, amidst thick grass beneath tall trees all was silent except for the twittering of birds.[18]

Showmen cared as much about the fate of their homeland as anyone; defence of kith and kin finding ready echo in hearts untroubled by ideology. But, they were engaged, too, in generations-long battles waged nearer at hand. Immediate restrictions on use of fuel and lighting and the nation's preoccupation with matters more serious than entertainment prompted authorities to cancel certain statutory fairs. Existence of chartered fairs depended on their taking place annually at the prescribed site. Should the fair fail to open on its special day at the time-hallowed place the charter lapsed.

Rumour went around that Chichester's Sloe Fair was endangered. How its charter was preserved by the actions of Joe's son-in-law is described in *Sussex Daily News*, 21 October 1939.

PIED POUDRE COURT
The Pied Poudre Court of the Bishops of Chichester, held at the annual Sloe Fair in medieval days, attracted citizens and folk from the surrounding countryside to the Fairground a few yards outside the North Gate in the City walls.

By ancient charter the Corporation of Chichester had provided since the days of the Henrys an open space for the merchants and showmen. The old days of horse-dealers, travelling wool and cloth merchants, and itinerant tradesmen in every commodity likely to tempt the fancy of the rural populations, have passed. But the booths and swings and sideshows continued, drawn to the ground in later years by powerful tractors and lorries. 'Walls of Death' have vied for popular favour with the modern thrills of the 'chairoplane' and bumper cars attracting townsmen and countrymen to the bright lights and 'hurdy-gurdy' of an up-to-date fair.

War-time has changed everything. A Sussex Daily News representative visited the ground in Northgate yesterday and found one stalwart of the showmen breed alone in the glory of his solitary coconut shy and darts alley. He was Mr Harry Stroud of Emsworth, sole defender of the ancient rights of the Showmen's Guild. By establishing one canvas-covered stall he has preserved for another year the privileges of the ancient charter.

Perhaps, who knows, the shades of the medieval showmen who set up their stalls at the old Pied Poudre Court held at Sloe Fair looked on with approval at a modern descendant 'doing his bit' while England once more is at war with her enemies?

Others, it seemed, did not rate Harry's achievement so highly. 'Whispered Confidences by the Batchelor' in the same newspaper a week later carried the lament:

SLOE FAIR
I now add another grudge to an already long list against Hitler. When in Chichester I do not expect anything to prevent my visit to Sloe Fair and look what happened this year. I hear that one school teacher used the belief that there was a fair on to get some children to go for a walk. My! Were they thrilled with the Coconut shy.

The Matthews family spent an anxious Christmas. Those not employed on A.R.P. work made some sort of living selling firewood. 'The Copse' in Steyning where they had left the loads was due to be ploughed early in Spring. They had been prevented from occupying their usual winter ground in Portsmouth through restrictions imposed on defence areas, but these did not apply to Shoreham where they opened the week after Easter, 1940.[19]

Gallopers and swing-boats had been transferred to St Giles' Meadow, Horsham, for storage, leaving just sideshows, Noah's Ark, and dodgems to open in the Adur Memorial Ground. The Boys used their

Joe and Ben Coneley on the gallopers. Joe married Rosie, Ben married Beatie Matthews.

ingenuity to screen the lighting by specially constructed shades and repainted the dodgem cars in silver and lake patterns so that they could be seen more distinctly in the dimmed lights. The whole fair was covered in with tilting, just a small opening being left for patrons to enter.[20] As another precaution, Amy's wagon and portable kitchen were painted in shades of camouflage green.[21]

Two of Amy's daughters had married the Coneley brothers, Ben and Joe, from a family of prominent Hampshire showmen. Since the roundabout was standing idle, it was agreed that they should have use of the ride until the end of the war. One day, when the Coneley fair was in full swing, Ben Coneley was alerted to the fact that the centre pole was shifting as the gallopers turned. It had worn thin and needed replacing. A visit to Dorset Iron Foundry brought no

Amy's grandchildren at Haywards Heath, 1947 (author on left; Tommy Matthews on right).

immediate joy. War requisitioning meant there was no iron to spare, but the foundryman did make a suggestion – why not improvise with a tall lamp standard? They took the advice and did exactly that. But the firebox and tubes had also worn thin and started to leak. The only solution was to change over from steam to electricity, so at last it came about that the famous steam-driven 'Electric Steeplechasers' were electrified!

Meanwhile, the Matthews brothers had moved their operations into Kent and East Sussex, continuing to open under blackout conditions. Amy often remained behind in her wagon at Battle while her sons took out the stuff. She was with them, however, when they travelled to Haywards Heath in May 1945 for a grand fund-raising fête held on behalf of the local hospital. There, on 8 May, they heard great news: the German army had surrendered.

Six months later J. Matthews & Sons brought dodgems, Noah's Ark, Park Swings, and sideshows to Essex Street, Brighton, for a fair to raise money for the Thank You Fund. The tober was a bombed site, its surface littered with broken bricks, tiles and fine dusty dirt left from crumpled houses. A little distance from where the stuff was built up, Amy's grandchildren were absorbed in play until distracted by a row going on – a row that for once had nothing to do with the showmen. The chavvies ran to see what was happening.

On a rougher part of the site where walls had been left standing a tinker was pulling down his tent after being ordered by the gavvers to move on. He growled and waved his fist at the town-children standing jeering as he dismantled his hovel. A boy called out some insult. The old man stopped dead, arms full of dingy canvas. He turned to face his tormentors and ... spat.

Their grandmother showed no emotion when the chavvies ran back and told her what they had just seen. Soon the tinker came shuffling past. Amy took two brown bottles from the belly-box under her wagon and slipped the beer into his handcart. She didn't know the old mush; was glad to see him gone. It did no good to the showmen to have tinkers or suchlike around when they were open. But, all the same, he was a traveller of sorts, he would appreciate something for the road.

Hove's Mayor ceremonially drove home the first stake of one of their sideshows when J. Matthews & Sons arrived in the town for victory carnival week in 1946.[22] Dodgems, Ark, swings, all the stalls were festooned with Union Jacks – but the gallopers had not been taken along. They were outmoded, had no place in a world chasing sensation spiced with danger

The gallopers on Ealing Common, 1947, after being sold to John Beach.

Sunny South, the Burrell, on Ealing Common, 1947 after being sold.

rather than phantasy. The following April the Boys sold the roundabout together with the Burrell engine, *Sunny South*, to Tom Beach of Ashford, Middlesex. Amy never set eyes on them again.

It was twelve years since Joe died. Amy, over seventy and slowing down, scolded herself for not getting round to doing half the things she used to do. Her hair, usually tucked up under a brimmed hat, was still sandy gold. The clothes she wore had hardly changed in style with the years – several pinafores layered on deep-waisted skirt, the pretty blouses with sleeves rolled up above her sinewy, bruised arms.

Although Amy, like all her contemporaries, had seen huge changes in three score years and ten, her way of life embodied massive forces of continuity. The round of her year still turned, as it always had, on the great fairs. Betweenwhiles, the family tended to take longer engagements at seaside resorts and, as village clubs were rendered redundant by the Welfare State, replaced them by flower shows, sports days and regattas. The dynamics of their lives were, as ever, determined by the annual fairs which culminated in the backend run: the Taro at Petersfield, Chichester's Sloe Fair, St Giles at Winchester, and then Petworth's Winter Fair.

As they approached the first of these in the autumn of 1949 it was clear that Amy was weary beyond telling. The Boys sent for their eldest sister, who urged her mother to go back with her for a few days' rest. Amy consented. Then the family knew something was very wrong. Louie and her husband had bought a shop during the war, settled down, become flatties. Amy had just agreed to leave her wagon to sleep under a house roof. It was understood from this that she was seriously ill.

After opening at Taro fair, with heavy hearts the Boys headed for Chichester and pulled into the Market Place. In her daughter's house, three days before Sloe Fair, Amy died quietly in her sleep.

Readers of *Southern Weekly*, 22 October 1949, were informed:

Today Sloe Fair is being held at Chichester, but one familiar face will be missing. Mrs Amy Matthews, a native of Guildford, 74, who has lived all her life in a caravan and is the widow of Mr Joseph Matthews, a member of the Showmen's Guild. She had attended most of the fairs on the south-east, south, and south-west coasts and was affectionately known as the 'Fair Queen'.

The funeral should have taken place today but to avoid creating depression among the patrons of Sloe Fair it has been put off until Monday.

On that day plants growing in Louie's garden were smothered by wreaths: a chair sculpted from flowers, horse shoes, gates of heaven, broken columns, a broken harp, crosses, cushions and baskets of blossoms. Among the wreaths the travellers stood talking in groups. Menfolk in black suits, weskets adorned with heavy gold chains, white scarves round their throats, flat caps on their heads; their ladies, handsomely dressed, lugubriously describing the trouble they'd had finding just the right shoes, or hat, to match their costume. Gold sovereigns gleamed, snared in brooches, pendants and bracelets; thin, brown, work-worn fingers were weighed down with flashy rings. Hundreds of people arrived to pay their respects – not just to Amy, not just to her family, but to the 'back life' that they all shared.

They went in their little groups to see the embalmed body. It was the custom. The front room of the house had been converted into a shrine. Crucifixes and candles arrayed against pure madonna lilies and in their midst, ageless now, in a white satin gown and her hair flowing loosely down over her shoulders, like a princess, Amy.

Gazing down at her, men and women wept. They mourned for the loss of Amy. She was loved and would be missed. They mourned for the passing of another generation, the like of which they would not see again.

Then they drove in long, slow procession to the church where they sang *Abide with me*. Each threw a handful of earth on to the coffin as it was lowered into the grave to lie beside Joe's.

At length they returned to where a huge marquee had been erected so that they could eat and drink and talk and talk together. The Boys, their wives, their sisters, brothers-in-law, the grandchildren, aunts, uncles, cousins, nieces and nephews, the Matthews clan all together.

The last of Amy's daughters to remain single had got married recently to Albert, son of Tom Smith, grandson of old Andrew. There were already more than a dozen grandchildren to carry on the family traditions. In the second half of the twentieth century many of the new generation would opt to settle down, become house-dwellers, but – there were enough chavvies in whose veins the blood of fairfield folk ran so strong that nothing would entice them to give up the road.

Street fair at Petworth – Joe's coconut shy built up.

POSTSCRIPT

On a sunny afternoon in October nearly half a century after the death of Amy Matthews, the streets of Chichester were lined with people waiting expectantly for the official opening of Sloe Fair. As the civic procession left the Council House in North Street, it was led by Chichester's Mayor and Mayoress, Councillor Barry Fletcher and his wife; the Chairman of Chichester District Council, Councillor Tony French; the Deputy Mayor, Councillor Eva French; and other dignitaries. It also included representatives of the Showmen's Guild of Great Britain; the Chief Steward of Sloe Fair, Lou Placito; the Chairman of the Fairground Association of Great Britain, Graham Downie; and several members of Amy's family. Upon reaching the Oakland's Way entrance to the fairground the procession stopped to allow a special ceremony to take place – the planting of a sloe tree by the Mayor assisted by Dr Henry Stroud. A plaque placed alongside the tree explained why it had been planted there:

During the dark days of World War II, showman Harry Stroud (1902-1968) defended the ancient traditions of Chichester's Sloe Fair. This sloe tree, planted by Chichester City Council on 20 October 1998, is dedicated to him so that today people may still enjoy 'All the Fun of the Fair'.

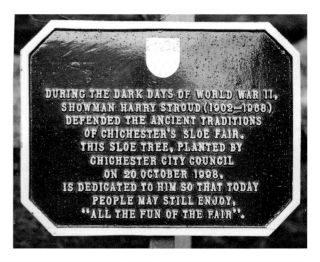

DURING THE DARK DAYS OF WORLD WAR II, SHOWMAN HARRY STROUD (1902–1968) DEFENDED THE ANCIENT TRADITIONS OF CHICHESTER'S SLOE FAIR. THIS SLOE TREE, PLANTED BY CHICHESTER CITY COUNCIL ON 20 OCTOBER 1998, IS DEDICATED TO HIM SO THAT TODAY PEOPLE MAY STILL ENJOY, "ALL THE FUN OF THE FAIR".

Planting the millennium tree at Chichester's Sloe Fair.

Harry and Louie Stroud's family at the ceremony.

This tree-planting ceremony had been organised by city councillor, Mrs Jennifer Wright, who said, 'I heard there was one chap that attended the Sloe Fair each year during the war and because he did that we kept our charter. I thought it was about time we said thank you.'

Among the attractions at Chichester that year were traditional rides such as Noyce's golden gallopers with its 89-key Gavioli organ, several faster rides – a Miami, Big Wheels, Orbiter, and a Waltzer, and scary shows such as the Castle of Horrors, a Haunted House, and a Mystic Maze. And where were Joe and Amy's nine sons and daughters in this busy throng? All but the youngest had long since gone, alas. Tom, the last surviving son, had died in 1987, aged 81, and been buried in Snodland, Kent, beside his wife Amy (née Bond). In latter years, too crippled by arthritis to decorate his family's rides, Tom had poured his heart into painting lively fairground scenes on canvas instead.

Below: Fairground scene painted by Thomas Matthews.

Tommy Matthews (1943-2001).

The Rock-o-Plane, an American ride bought by Tommy in 1981.

Mirrored shields engraved with Joe Matthews's initials.

Tommy's Rotor.

Of the seventeen grandchildren who survived Joe and Amy, Tom's son – another Tom – was the only one destined to grow up and keep the name of Matthews. Born at Hurst Green in East Sussex on 1 June 1943 and descended on both sides from generations of travelling showpeople, he had already made a name for himself before Tom senior's death. Despite mourning the fact that he had not inherited his father's talent as an artist, any skill he lacked with a paintbrush the younger Tom (Tommy) more than made up for with his creativity as designer and manufacturer of fairground rides. Inspired by the same ambition that had inspired his grandfather and great grandfather – he wanted to be the proprietor of one of the big rides on the fairground. He especially dreamt of possessing the set of gallopers that Joe and his sons had refurbished, with its horses each named for the family. Although in the ownership of a different family now, its rounding boards still bore the mirrored shields engraved with the proud initials *JM* – Joseph Matthews. Tommy Matthews dreamed of buying back that roundabout.

His first venture into the realm of fairground rides, however, was not connected with gallopers, but with a very different ride. In 1976 Tommy, married to Dorothy (née Whittle) and father of three young children, was casting around for a means to support his family. He decided that what he needed was a reliable ride that was easy to build up and completely different from anything already operating at the fairs he was due to visit. The trouble was, new rides cost a lot of money – probably more than a young family man could afford. So, what to do? He came up with a characteristic answer. If he wanted such a ride, he would have to build it himself. Rising at six every morning to put in two hours of construction work before getting changed to mind his stalls at Great Yarmouth Pleasure Beach, after two seasons he was ready to reveal his new machine – a Rotor, a show in which riders were spun against the inner walls of a cylinder as the floor dropped away to leave them pinned against the walls by centripetal force. Aimed to attract spectators as well as riders, it was an instant success. But the clue to Tommy's future achievements as a manufacturer lay in the fact that he had designed his Rotor to be compact enough to travel as one load. The consequent saving in time, fuel and man-power became the hallmark of his later products.

Having succeeded with the Rotor, Tommy turned his attention to another traditional ride that was due for a make-over. The Ghost Train, popular on British fairgrounds since the mid-nineteenth century, was now going out of fashion because it was cumbersome and too difficult to build up and pull down on many grounds. Putting his mind to these problems, Tommy came up with the Roller Ghosta, and by making it less of a show and more of a thrill ride found a way of having spectators up-front to attract more custom.

Next, Tommy set about developing the Tri-Star, a ride that was already popular, especially with teenagers. Soon his version became a familiar sight on fairgrounds in the Home Counties and began to be exported abroad. By the turn of the millennium, he

had designed and built three Rotors, more than twenty Miamis, a double-decker Glasshouse, six Tristars, three double-decker Rollerghostas, a Wave Swinger, and two sets of fold-up Dodgems.

But despite this success with fast modern rides, it was the gallopers, icon of the fairground, that still beckoned. Given a choice, Tommy would have bought back his grandfather's set that had been sold after the War and was now in the ownership of prominent showman, Bobby Rawlins. Realising that the asking price must be too high, Tommy again fell back on his own resources. If he could not have his grandfather's gallopers, he said, then he would have to make a set of his own. And this was exactly what he did. Not to the same pattern, though. Drawing on years of experience, he produced the first one-load set of gallopers to travel English roads, and to a design simple enough to be built up in the shortest time. Their first appearance was on Brighton beach in front of the Palace pier where Tommy opened them for three summer seasons as well as taking them to Hereford market place each Christmas. Six sets of gallopers followed. Of these, one went to Barry Island, the next to Skegness, a fourth to Rhyl. But by the time he came to design the seventh, Tommy was faced with a special challenge. In 1999 the Royal Parks Agency in London was looking for a showman to operate a set of gallopers in Hyde Park. After the concession was won by Bob Wilson's funfairs, they immediately put in an order for a new set of gallopers from Tommy. He responded with a splendid set featuring royal coaches instead of chariots, and a rounding board decorated with famous London scenes.

Tommy's one load set of gallopers, designed to be built up at a low level before being lifted from the centre into position.

First set of gallopers designed by Tommy, built up on Brighton seafront.

John Simons taking delivery of Tommy's fourth set of gallopers at Rhyl.

Tommy's second set of gallopers on the Sandringham estate.

The London Zoo set of gallopers.

Tommy's seventh set of gallopers, the Hyde Park set.

Tommy's gallopers open at Covent Garden, December 2002.

Above: Close-up of dragon chariot.

Left: Horses named after Tommy's sons.

Below: Knebworth House Music Festival
– first time open.

Sadly, Tommy, great-great grandson of Chewbacca Matthews, died at the height of his creative powers in September 2001, leaving his third set of fold-up Dodgems to be completed by his sons Tommy III and Perrin Matthews who not only saw the job through but continued to develop their father's business. They also continue to visit many of the fairs that the Matthews family have been attending for the past two hundred years and more. So, although the forces of change are obvious, especially in the showmen's new forms of transport and up-to-date amusements, equally evident are the enduring rhythms and massive forces of continuity embodied in their lives. While it

is recognised that many of our traditional fairs are still held on the same day in the same place as they have been for centuries, it may come as a surprise to find that their attractions are often provided by members of the same families who have attended them for hundreds of years. Indeed, there can't be many fairgrounds in the south country today where one would not come across some of Chewbacca and Liddy Matthews's descendants, people whose destinies hung by such a slender thread in that desperate winter of 1836. Then again, perhaps we should not be so surprised, for such is the resilience of Britain's fairfield folk.

Hayley and John Leonard in front of their mother's Rolldown. Setting out her stall is Ruby Leonard, daughter of Annie and Alf Bond, granddaughter of Joe and Amy Matthews, another branch of the family who proudly maintain its time-honoured traditions.

Ruby with her grandson, John Leonard, at Looe, Cornwall, in 2007.

Baby Regan with his three-year old brother John in their Silver Cross prams at Haresfield, Gloucestershire. They are great, great, great, great grandsons of Chewbacca and Liddy Matthews.

Left: Carmen and Sharon Leonard.

143

APPENDIX

Steam engines owned by showmen mentioned in the text

BURRELL

Burrell No. 1470 (1890) 7 nhp. Sold new to G.& T. **Bartlett** (Fordingbridge, Hants) who named her *Pride of the South*. With Richard Chipperfield (Redditch) by 1922.

Burrell No. 1628 (1892) 8 nhp. Reg. No. CF 3634. Single crank compound engine. Built as a road locomotive and sold to E.P. Bailey (Cranbrook, Kent) In 1894 converted by Burrell into showman's engine and sold to **Joseph Matthews** (Haslemere, Surrey) Sold in 1904 to Charles Barnes (Great Ryburgh, Norfolk) who named her *Royal Hunter*. Sold out of showland in 1918.

Burrell No. 1674 (1893) 8 nhp. Road locomotive sold new to **John Harris** (Cuckfield, Sussex), in April, 1893 and named *Masterpiece*.

Burrell No.1909 (1896) Sold new to G.& T. **Bartlett** (Fordingbridge, Hants) who named her *Majestic*. By 1901 sold on to Jacob Studt (Pontypridd) and later with W.Gritt, 1925

Burrell No.2134 (1898) 10 nhp. Reg.No. BW 6546. compound engine. Built as a road locomotive and sold to A.Wickens (Reading). After two more owners, sold to **Tom Smith** (Shoreham, Sussex) who converted her to a showman's engine and named her *Wanderer*. Scrapped in 1950.

Burrell No. 3194 (1910) 4 nhp. Sold new to **William Matthews** (Farnborough, Hants) who named it *St Bernard*.

Burrell No. 3239 (1910) 7 nhp. Reg. No. BP 5497. New to C.M.Fox (Marden, Kent), later to Dan and Stone Ltd. Of Hartlip (Kent). By 1921 with Frank Duke Ltd of Steyning. About 1939 sold to **Matthews** and used as showman's engine. In 1951 sold to J.W.Hardwick, scrap dealer in West Ewell, Surrey.

Burrell No. 3542 (1914) 6 nhp. Reg. No. NO 472. Compound engine. Built as a road locomotive and sold new to James Penna & Sons (Cornwall), then on to John Sadd & Sons (Essex) Converted by Openshaw (Reading) to a showman's engine and in 1929 sold to **Joseph Matthews** (Sussex) who named it *Sunny South*. In 1947 sold to John Beach (Middlesex) and scrapped c.1957.

Burrell No. 3660 (1915) 6 nhp. Reg. No. HT3244. Named *Victor*. Road locomotive, new to James Jennings (Trowbridge, Wiltshire). 1919 sold to D.Harrison (Bristol). 1927 sold to F.Oldridge (Plymouth). 1928 purchased by **Joe Rowland** (St Austell, Cornwall). Scrapped early 1950s.

Burrell No. 3732 (1916) 4 nhp. Sold to **Tom Smith** (Shoreham, Sussex)

Burrell No. No.3869 (1920) Reg. No. FJ1514. New to Exeter Corporation. In 1930 sold to Charles Openshaw (Reading) who converted it to showman's type. Sold to Hibble & Mellor (Nottingham). 1935 bought by Smith Bros. (Plymouth) who named it *City of Plymouth*. Later acquired by **Joe Rowland.**

FODEN

Foden No.528 (1902) Reg. No. BP6589. Road locomotive sold to the Royal Engineers at Chatham. By 1910 bought by William Beach (Hammersmith) who converted her into a showman's engine and named her *George V*. Sold to **Tom Smith** in 1921. Renamed *Pride of the South*. Scrapped in 1949.

Foden No.6494 Reg. No. M8860. Five tonner bought from B. Heath (Guildford) by **Matthews** in 1925. Sold to J. Brown & Son (Shoreham, Sussex).

Foden No.11000 (1923) new to **Matthews** and registered through Foden agent, J.Kiln of Cosham, who registered it in Portsmouth as either BK8503 or 8653. Later to J.Penfold (Barnham) who scrapped it.

Foden No.12236 (1926) Six tonner, ex-wagon, new to R.Bush, Thatcham. Purchased by **Matthews** by 1935. Last licensed in 1938.

Foden No. 12366. Reg. No. PX4545. Six-tonner ex-wagon new to Parson Bros. (Shoreham) and then to **Matthews**. Not licensed, possibly used for spares.

Foden No. 12386 (1926) Reg. No. PM7084. Ex-wagon 6-tonner tractor on pneumatics. New to C.Packham (Hurstpierpoint). Sold to **Joseph Matthews** in 1939, then to J.W.Hardwick & Sons and scrapped in 1951.

FOWLER

Fowler No. 9456 (1902) Reg. No. KK 3634. A4/R compound engine. Built as a road locomotive and sold to Robert Cann of Wareham, Dorset. After several more owners, sold to **Tom Smith** who converted her into a showman's engine and named her *Marina*. Later sold out of showland.

Fowler No.13047 (1914) 10 nhp. Reg. No. DP3863. B6 compound engine. Built as a road locomotive and sold new to the War Department. After 1918 converted by Charles Openshaw (Reading) into a showman's engine and in 1928 sold to **Joseph Matthews** (Worthing) who named her *Wanderer*. Sold c.1947 to James Foster, timber merchant (Emsworth). Scrapped in mid-1950s by Pollock Brown & Co. (Southampton)

Fowler No. 14113 (1914) Road locomotive new to the War Department. After 1918 **William Matthews** bought it to replace the engine he had lost and named it *The Lion*.

GARRETT

Garrett No.33739 (1919) Reg. No. BJ4803. Named *Endeavour*. 4CD type tractor, new to Edison Steam Rolling Co. (Dorchester). Later to Newland & Co. (Bournemouth). In 1933 bought by Reuben Gilham (Southampton), who converted it to a showman's tractor. In 1934 sold to **Joe Rowland**. Scrapped after 1941.

SAVAGE

Savage (1888) **William Matthews** ordered 'one 6 nhp traction engine, 8 ins. bore x 10 ins. stroke; fitted with steel relieving gear'. A Savage single-cylinder traction engine named *Queen Elizabeth* was in his possession in September 1915.

TASKER

Tasker 1342 (1905) Reg. No. AA 2025. B1 three-ton compound tractor kept in stock until 1908. Sold to C.J.Newbury & Sons, (Warsash, Hants). By 1921 bought by **Joseph Matthews** (Worthing) who named it *Mighty Atom*.

Tasker 1406 (1909) Reg.No. BP 5705. B2 five-ton compound engine. New to Wakefield Bros. (Nutbourne, Sussex). Returned to Taskers in 1923 and resold to **Matthews** who named her *Speed Princess*.

Tasker 1431 (1910) Reg. No. AA2371. Bought from French (Seaford, Sussex) by **Rowland Bros.** (St Austell) in 1921. Named *Princess Mary*. Sold for scrap in 1941.

Tasker 1595 (1914), Reg. No. AA 5264. B2 five ton compound tractor, sold new to Weymouth Steam Haulage Co., then on to Hall & Co. (Worthing), before being purchased by **Joseph Matthews** (West Worthing) who converted her to showman's tractor and named her *Pride of Sussex*. Scrapped by her last owners, Robert & Gardiner (Stamford, Lincs.) in 1953.

Tasker 1596 (1914), Reg. No. AA 5262. B2 compound tractor, sold to F.W.Bloomfield (Wymering, Hants), then on to Mrs J. Smith (Southampton) who converted her into a showman's tractor before selling to **Jerry Russett** & Sons (Southampton) who named her *King of the Road*.

Tasker 1770 (1919) Reg. No. HO 2285. B2 compound tractor, sold to Holloway Bros. (Liverpool), then to Box & Turner (Ardingly, Sussex) before being bought by **Tom Smith** (Shoreham, Sussex) and used for haulage only, not fitted with a dynamo. Sold on and last registered in 1947.

NOTES

Chapter One
[1] Sanger, 'Lord' George, *Seventy Years a Showman* (1926), 121-3.
[2] *West Sussex Gazette*, 27 May 1869.

Chapter Two
[1] *Sussex County Magazine*, 1953 Vol.XXVII, 216.
[2] *West Sussex Gazette*, 7 June 1860.
[3] *West Sussex Gazette*, 28 June 1860.
[4] A. Macnaghten, *Windsor in Victorian Times* (1975), 24.
[5] *Windsor and Eton Express*, 30 Oct.1847.
[6] *Windsor & Eton Express,* 27 Oct.1855.
[7] *Windsor & Eton Express* 25 Oct.1856.
[8] *World's Fair*, 25 Sept. 1920.
[9] *West Sussex Gazette*, 5 Aug.1869.
[10] *Daily Mail*, 6 Sept,1897,
[11] *Barnet Press*, 12 Sept.1874.
[12] *Barnet Press*, 10 Sept.1870.
[13] A. Macnaghten: *Windsor in Victorian Times* (1975), 52.
[14] *Windsor and Eton Express,* 1 Nov. 1862.

Chapter Three
[1] *West Sussex Gazette*, 2 June 1870.
[2] *World's Fair*, 25 Sept. 1920.
[3] G.Sturt, *A Small Boy in the Sixties* (Hassocks,1977). Showmen used two different sorts of stake for driving in their coconut shies: metal ones for cobbled streets and wooden ones for grass.
[4] E.R.Pennell, *Charles Godrey Leland*, 155-6.
[5] J. Challacombe, *Jottings from a Farnborough Notebook* (1922).
[6] *Windsor & Eton Express*, 31Oct.1863.
[7] *Windsor & Eton Express*, 28 Oct.1865.
[8] *Windsor & Eton Express*, 26 Oct.1867.
[9] *West Sussex Gazette*, 25 Nov.1875.
[10] *West Sussex Gazette* 24 Nov.1881.
[11] *West Sussex Gazette* 24 Nov.1881.
[12] *West Sussex Gazette* 7 May1874.
[13] *Sheldrake's Aldershot & Sandhurst Military Gazette*, 8 July 1882.
[14] *Surrey & Hants News*, 4 Aug.1883.

Chapter Four
[1] *West Sussex Gazette*, 10June1869.
[2] *West Sussex Gazette*, 28 Jan. 1886.

[3] *West Sussex Gazette*, 28 June 1883.
[4] *West Sussex Gazette*, 25 Nov. 1886.
[5] *Surrey & Hants News*, 23July 1887.
[6] Ewbank Smith, *Victorian Farnham* (Chichester, 1971),149.
[7] *Surrey & Hants News*, 29 June 1901.
[8] *Surrey & Hants News*, 15 Nov.1902.

Chapter Five
[1] *Sheldrake's Aldershot Military Gazette*, 22 Aug. 1902.
[2] *Sheldrake's Aldershot Military Gazette*, 22 July 1904.
[3] *World's Fair*, 25 Sept. 1920.
[4] *Sheldrake's Aldershot Military Gazette*, 21June 1907.
[5] *South Bucks Standard, 20 Sept. 1907*
[6] *South Bucks Standard*, 28 Sept. 1906.
[7] *World's Fair*, 25 Sept. 1920.
[8] *The Herald*, 8 Aug. 1908.
[9] *The Herald*, 22 Aug. 1908.
[10] *The Herald*, 7 Aug. 1909.
[11] *Sheldrake's Aldershot Military Gazette*, 10 June 1910.
[12] *Richmond & Twickenham Times*, 10 June 1911.
[13] *Richmond Herald*, 22 June 1911.
[14] *Sheldrake's Aldershot Military Gazette*, 2 June 1911.
[15] *Sheldrake's Aldershot Military Gazette*, 30 June 1911.
[16] *Sheldrake's Aldershot Military Gazette*, 21 July 1911.
[17] *Sheldrake's Aldershot Military Gazette*, 28 June 1912.
[18] *The South Bucks Standard*, 25 Sept. 1913.
[19] *Royal Military College Magazine*, Michaelmas Term,1919.
[20] *Royal Military College Magazine*, Michaelmas Term,1921.
[21] *Aldershot Gazette & Military News*, Sept. 1920.
[22] *Aldershot Gazette & Military News*, 23 Feb. 1922.

Chapter Six
[1] *West Sussex Gazette*, 12 July 1860.
[2] *West Sussex Gazette*, 28 July 1859.
[3] *West Sussex Gazette*, 22 Oct. 1863.
[4] *West Sussex Gazette*, 11 May 1865.

5 *West Sussex Gazette*, 16 Aug. 1866.
6 *West Sussex Gazette*, 23 April 1868.
7 *West Sussex Gazette*, 9 Oct. 1862.
8 *West Sussex Gazette*, 6 Oct. 1859.
9 *West Sussex Gazette*, 4 Oct. 1877.
10 *West Sussex Gazette*, 16 May 1867.
11 *West Sussex Gazette*, 7 May 1868.
12 *West Sussex Gazette*, 22 Oct. 1868.
13 *West Sussex Gazette*, 14 Aug. 1862.
14 *West Sussex Gazette*, 2 Dec. 1869.
15 *West Sussex Gazette*, 1 Oct. 1863.
16 *West Sussex Gazette*, 9 July 1874.
17 *West Sussex Gazette*, 26 Oct. 1865.
18 *West Sussex Gazette* 13 July 1871.
19 *West Sussex Gazette*, 25 July 1872.
20 *West Sussex Gazette*, 23 July 1874.
21 *West Sussex Gazette*, 23 July 1874.
22 *West Sussex Gazette*, 13 Aug. 1874.
23 *West Sussex Gazette*, 12 April 1883.
24 *West Sussex Gazette*, 19 April 1883.
25 *West Sussex Gazette*, 9 April 1885.
26 *West Sussex Gazette*, 4 Aug. 1864.

Chapter Seven
1 *West Sussex Gazette*, 27 Nov. 1856.
2 *West Sussex Gazette*, 26 Nov. 1868.
3 *West Sussex Gazette*, 5 Nov. 1908.
4 *West Sussex Gazette*, 24 Feb. 1876.
5 *West Sussex Gazette*, 14 June 1877.
6 *West Sussex Gazette*, 26 July 1877.
7 *West Sussex Gazette*, 4 Aug. 1887.
8 *West Sussex Gazette*, 12 June 1902.
9 *West Sussex Gazette*, 19 June 1902.
10 *West Sussex Gazette*, 31 July 1902.
11 *West Sussex Gazette*, 11 June 1903.
12 *West Sussex Gazette*, 10 Nov. 1904.
13 *West Sussex Gazette*, 26 Nov. 1908.
14 *West Sussex Gazette*, 6 April 1905.
15 *West Sussex Gazette*, 26 Oct. 1905.
16 *West Sussex Gazette*, 9 Nov. 1905.
17 *West Sussex Gazette*, 25 July 1907.
18 *West Sussex Gazette*, 11 June 1908.
19 *West Sussex Gazette*, 29 July 1909.
20 *West Sussex Gazette*, 25 May 1916.
21 *West Sussex Gazette*,17 Aug. 1916.
22 *West Sussex Gazette*, 24 Aug. 1916.
23 *West Sussex Gazette*, 22 Feb. 1917.
24 *West Sussex Gazette*, 29 July 1937.

Chapter Eight
1 *West Sussex Gazette*,16 Dec. 1858.
2 *West Sussex Gazette*, 8 Aug. 1867.
3 *West Sussex Gazette*, 25 March 1875.
4 *West Sussex Gazette*, 22 July 1875.

5 *World's Fair*, 18 Sept. 1948.
6 *West Sussex Gazette*, 15 May 1879.
7 *West Sussex Gazette*, 19 June 1879.
8 *West Sussex Gazette*, 26 June 1879.
9 *West Sussex Gazette*, 31 July 1879.
10 *West Sussex Gazette*, 20 May 1880.
11 *West Sussex Gazette*, 2 June 1881.
12 *West Sussex Gazette*, 4 Aug. 1883.
13 *West Sussex Gazette*, 8, 17 & 24 July 1884.
14 *West Sussex Gazette*, 9 Oct. 1884.
15 *West Sussex Gazette*, 14 & 28 July 1887.

Chapter Nine
1 *West Sussex Gazette*, 22 Nov. 1888.
2 *West Sussex Gazette*, 31 July 1890.
3 *West Sussex Gazette*, 25 May 1893.
4 *West Sussex Gazette*, 14 Sept.1893.
5 *West Sussex Gazette*, 23 May 1895.
6 *West Sussex Gazette*, 30 May & 6 June 1895.
7 *West Sussex Gazette*, 18 Nov. 1886.
8 *West Sussex Gazette*, 23 Dec. 1886.
9 *West Sussex Gazette*, 12 Feb. 1891.
10 *West Sussex Gazette*, 11 Aug. 1898.
11 *West Sussex Gazette*, 20 April 1899.
12 *West Sussex Gazette*, 13 July 1899.
13 *West Sussex Gazette*, 3 Aug. 1899.
14 *West Sussex Gazette*, 10 Aug. 1899.
15 *West Sussex Gazette*, 17 May 1900.
16 *West Sussex Gazette*, 31 May 1900.
17 *West Sussex Gazette*, 12 July 1900.
18 *West Sussex Gazette*, 30 May 1901.
19 *West Sussex Gazette*, 12 Oct. 1901.
20 *West Sussex Gazette*, 26 Oct. 1901.
21 *West Sussex Gazette*, 19 June 1902.
22 *West Sussex Gazette*, 31 July 1902.
23 *West Sussex Gazette*, 23 Oct. 1902.
24 *West Sussex Gazette*, 29 Oct. 1903.
25 *West Sussex Gazette*, 29 May 1902.
26 WSRO Pol w/w/1/5-7.
27 *West Sussex Gazette*, 28 May 1903.
28 *West Sussex Gazette*, 7 Nov. 1907.
29 *West Sussex Gazette*, 24 March 1904.
30 *West Sussex Gazette*, 27 Oct. 1904.
31 *West Sussex Gazette*, 26 Oct.1905.
32 *West Sussex Gazette*, 27 July 1905.
33 *West Sussex Gazette*, 17 May 1906.
34 *World's Fair*, 9 Nov.1907.
35 *West Sussex Gazette*,15 July 1909.

Chapter Ten
1 *West Sussex Gazette*, 30 July 1868.
2 *Dorset County Chronicle*, 17 Oct. 1895.
3 *Dorset County Chronicle*, 24 Oct. 1895.
4 *Dorset County Chronicle*, 15 Oct. 1896.

5 *West Sussex Gazette,* 4 April 1907; *World's Fair,* 13 April 1907.
6 *World's Fair* 30 March 1929.
7 *World's Fair* 20 Dec. 1913.
8 *West Sussex Gazette,* 7 July 1910.
9 *West Sussex Gazette,* 27 June 1912.
10 *West Sussex Gazette,* 12 Sept. 1912.
11 *West Sussex Gazette,* 24 Oct. 1912.
12 *West Sussex Gazette,* 3 & 10 July 1913.
13 *World's Fair,* 7 Sept. 1907.
14 *West Sussex Gazette,* 15 Aug. 1907.
15 *West Sussex Gazette,* 20 Aug. 1914.
16 *West Sussex Gazette,* 2 Nov. 1914.
17 *West Sussex Gazette,* 12 Aug. 1915.
18 *West Sussex Gazette,* 17 Aug. 1916.
19 *West Sussex Gazette,* 15 Aug. 1918.
20 *West Sussex Gazette,* 12 Aug. 1920.
21 *West Sussex Gazette,* 31 May 1923.
22 *World's Fair,* 17 & 31 May 1924.
23 *World's Fair,* 11 Sept. 1926.
24 *World's Fair,* 11 Dec. 1926.
25 *World's Fair,* 14 April 1928.

Chapter Eleven
1 *World's Fair,* 13 April 1929.
2 *World's Fair,* 1 June 1929.
3 *World's Fair,* 29 June 1929.
4 *World's Fair,* 27 July 1929.
5 *World's Fair,* 10 Aug.1929.
6 *World's Fair,* 11 Jan.1930.
7 *World's Fair,* 3 May 1930.
8 *Nottinghamshire Weekly Express*, 26 June 1891.
9 *World's Fair,* 28 May 1932.
10 *World's Fair,* 27 Aug. 1932.

11 *World's Fair,* 3 Dec. 1932.
12 *World's Fair,* 15 April 1933.
13 *World's Fair,* 27 May 1933.
14 *World's Fair,* 3 June 1933.
15 *World's Fair,* 5 Aug. 1933.
16 *World's Fair,* 28 Oct. 1933.
17 *World's Fair,* 17 March 1934.
18 *World's Fair,* 21 April 1934.
19 *World's Fair,* 22 Sept. 1934.
20 *World's Fair,* 15 Dec. 1934.

Chapter 12
1 *World's Fair,* 17 Aug. 1935.
2 *World's Fair,* 31 Aug. 1935.
3 *World's Fair,* 31 Aug. 1935.
4 *World's Fair,* 11 April 1936.
5 *World's Fair,* 19 Sept. 1936.
6 *World's Fair,* 3 April 1937.
7 *World's Fair,* 12 June 1937.
8 *World's Fair,* 10 July 1937.
9 *World's Fair,* 24 July 1937.
10 *World's Fair,* 18 Sept.1937.
11 *World's Fair,* 16 Oct. 1937.
12 *World's Fair,* 18 March 1939.
13 *World's Fair,* 1 April 1939.
14 *World's Fair,* 15 April 1939.
15 *World's Fair,* 13 May 1939.
16 *World's Fair,* 15 July 1939.
17 *World's Fair,* 12 Aug. 1939.
18 *World's Fair,* 16 Sept. 1939.
19 *World's Fair,* 11 May 1939.
20 *World's Fair,* 25 May 1939.
21 *World's Fair,* 15 June 1939.
22 *World's Fair,* 15 June 1946.

GLOSSARY

Atchin-tan	A camping place	Dolls	Game of Aunt Sally
Back-end run	End-of-season fairs	Domes	Carved decoration surmounting rounding board
Bickin	Hawking		
Biddi	Little	Dordy	Oh dear!
Bioscope	Early travelling cinema	Dosh	Money
Centre engine	Motor which drives roundabout	Droppers, drops	Carved decoration suspended from rounding board
Centre truck	Wheeled framework of centre engine	Duveleste	God's sake
		Fizzer-seller	Hawker of sherbert and fruit to troops on the march
Chairoplanes	Suspended chairs which swing out as the ride turns		
		Flat, flattie	Non-showman
Chap	Manual labourer employed by showmen	Gaff	Fairground site
Chavvy, chavvies	Child, children	Gallopers	Galloping horse roundabout
Cheap jack	Travelling hawker	Glasshouse	Spooky themed walk-through or ride-through attraction
Club Day	Annual festivity, often share-out of Benefit Society funds		
		Gorgies	Non-travellers
Dandy	Wheeled water tank	Gavver	Policeman
Didikai	Half-breed gypsy, or rough fellow	Hedge mumper	Tramp
		Hoopla	Game where rings are thrown over prizes
Dinilow	Daft		
Dobbies	Wooden horse roundabout, hand driven or worked by pony	Jukel	Dog
		Junkers	Rushes
Dodgems	Cars powered by overhead electric grid	Kipsey-doeser	Basket maker
		Knock-'em-downs	Throwing game where prizes are dislodged from stand
Dodger	Small besom for sweeping hearth		
		Kushti	Good
Doings	Money takings	Livetts	Sticks for shying at coconuts

Miami	16 seater ride where seats swing from side to side at random	**Rye**	Gentleman
Mill	Bare-fist fight	**Snuff box sticks**	Throwing game where snuff boxes are prizes to be dislodged
Mochardi	Taboo	**Striker**	Game where player hits peg with mallet to send striker soaring towards high bell
Mooey	Face		
Mullerin	Dying	**Stuff**	Generic term for fairground amusements
Mulo-mush	Death		
Munjari	To eat, food	**Swag**	Fairground prizes
Mush	Man	**Swift**	Radial spokes supporting spinning frame of roundabout
Naphtha flare	Oil lamp	**Switchback**	Undulating track roundabout
Needies	Low caste travellers	**Tilt**	Canvas covering rides and fairground shows
Parney	Urine		
Poovin the grais	Grazing the horses	**Tober**	Fairground
Rakli	Girl	**Touch 'ems**	Game like skittles
Riding master	Owner of rides who sublets ground to other showmen	**Trashed**	Frightened
		Tri-Star	A simple spin and swoop ride
Ringing the changes	Money swindle, where confusion is caused by giving and retracting a succession of coins	**U.K.S.V.D.A**	United Kingdom Showmen & Van Dwellers' Association
		Wave Swinger	Chairoplane-type ride on which the rotating top also tilts
Rollerghosta	Cross between ghost train and thrill ride that caters for spectators	**Welting**	Beating, punishment
		Wheel-'em-in	Circular stall where pennies are rolled on to a chequered board
Rotor	Rotating drum that pins riders to the wall		
Rounding board	Decorated board embellishing the top of a roundabout		

SOURCES

NEWSPAPERS AND MAGAZINES

Barnet Press
Brighton Gazette
Brighton Herald
Chichester Observer
The Cornishman
Daily Mail
Dorset County Chronicle
Farnham Herald
Hampshire Chronicle
Romsey Journal
Journal of the Gypsy Lore Society
Richmond Herald
Richmond & Twickenham Times
Royal Military College Record
Sheldrake's Aldershot Military Gazette

South Bucks Standard
South of England Advertiser
Surrey Advertiser
Surrey & Hants News
Sussex Advertiser
Sussex County Magazine
Sussex Daily News
West Sussex Gazette
West Sussex Journal
West Sussex Observer
Winchester Observer
Windsor & Eton Express
World's Fair
Worthing Gazette

BIBLIOGRAPHY

Baker, Margaret. DISCOVERING ENGLISH FAIRS (Shires Publications. 1965)

Bede's HISTORY OF THE ENGLISH CHURCH & PEOPLE (Penguin, 1955)

Braithwaite, David. SAVAGE OF KING'S LYNN (Patrick Stephens, 1975)

Braithwaite, David. TRAVELLING FAIRS (Shire Publications, 1976)

Brent, Colin and Rector, William. VICTORIAN LEWES (Phillimore, 1980)

Challacombe, Jessie. JOTTINGS FROM A FARNBOROUGH NOTEBOOK (Gale & Polden, 1922)

Cole, Lieut-Colonel H.N. THE STORY OF ALDERSHOT (Gale & Polden, 1951)

Crawley, John. FAIRGROUND ENGINES IN FOCUS (John Crawley, 1983)

Dallas, Duncan. THE TRAVELLING PEOPLE (Macmillan, 1971)

Dexter, T.F.C. THE PAGAN ORIGIN OF FAIRS (New Knowledge Press, 1930)

Jerrome, P., and Newdick, J. PETWORTH: THE WINDS OF CHANGE (The Window Press, 1983)

Leigh, Rhoda. PAST & PASSING (Heath Cranton, 1932)

Leland, C.C. THE ENGLISH GYPSIES AND THEIR LANGUAGE (Kegan Paul, Trench, Trubner, 1893)

Pennell, E.R. CHARLES CODFREY LELAND (Houghton, Mifflin, 1906)

Roope, F.C. COME TO THE FAIR (The Showmen's Guild, 1961)

Sanger, 'Lord' George. SEVENTY YEARS A SHOWMAN (J.M. Dent & Sons, 1926)

Smith, Ewbank. VICTORIAN FARNHAM (Phillimore, 1971)

Sturt, George. A SMALL BOY IN THE SIXTIES (Harvester Press, 1977)

ACKNOWLEDGEMENTS

Undoubtedly the most enjoyable part of my research involved meeting and conversing with many people connected with today's travelling fairs. I am grateful to them all for being so generous with their time and hospitality. In particular I should like to thank:

Mr A. Bond, Mr & Mrs B. Coneley, Mr B. Coneley (Pirbright), Mr R. Cothard, Miss L. Davis, Mrs R. Leonard, Mrs H. Matthews, Mr T. H. Matthews, Mrs J. Noyce, Mr R. Rawlins, Mr & Mrs F. Rowland, Mrs P. Smith, Mrs J. Toomey, Miss P. Turner, Mr J. Wall.

I should like to express my gratitude to the following for allowing me to use photographs in their possession:

Mr C.P. Barnes, Mr P.W. Bradley, Mr C. Castle, Mr D. Cleeve, Mr B. Colbourne, Mrs B. Coneley, Mrs R. Leonard, Mrs W. Matthews, Mrs J. Ramsey, Mr R. Smith, Mrs N. Smitheram, Mr B. D. Stoyel, Miss B.L. Stroud, the late Mr H.J.F. Thompson, the late Mrs H. Turner, Mrs J. Wall.

Other photographs are by courtesy of:

Aldershot Military Museum; Chichester District Museum; Fairground Postcard Society; the Museum of Farnham; Haslemere Educational Museum; St Nicholas Church, Wickham; Sussex Archaeological Society; West Sussex Record Office.

I am also grateful to the Fairground Association of Great Britain and the Southern Counties Historic Vehicle Preservation Trust who provided help and information.

Finally, I must pay tribute to my husband without whose support and encouragement this book would never have been written.

These acknowledgements, written when the book was first published more than twenty years ago, have not been adjusted in this edition, but I should like to add my thanks to all those who have helped and encouraged me in the production of this new edition. In particular I should like to thank my brother, Dr Henry Stroud, the late Mr Ernie Taylor, the Romany and Traveller Family History Society, Keith Colbourne, Graham Downie, Kerry Hawkins, Mr S. G. Knight, Ruby and Hayley Leonard, Dorothy Matthews and family, Robert Dane Matthews, John Reeves, Trevor and Foronda Smith, and Roy Snelling.

INDEX